SHORT STACK PUBLISHING

HOW TO HANDLE LIVING YOUR DOG

D1350177

Winkie lives in SW London with her two dogs,
Dennis, an ex rescue Parsons Jack Russell and her lurcher,
Maisie. After many office bound years in the corporate world she
now works full-time as a dog trainer and behaviourist and is a
practising Bowen Therapist for both people and dogs.
In addition Winkie plans and conducts talks and seminars on
various dog related subjects both in the UK and Europe.

Her views and lifestyle are holistic and
she consistently strives to update her skills
and expand her professional knowledge in all areas.
Her aim in life is to improve the general understanding and
knowledge of dogs to the mutual benefit of both dogs and their
owners. She seeks to dispel the myths and outdated ideas that
can have a negative impact on our relationship with dogs.
In all dog related matters she works actively with vets
to ensure that she provides an informed and
balanced view on dog related issues.

Her goal with *this* book is, of course, to help you discover
How to Handle Living With Your Dog

To find out more about Winkie and her puppy classes, Canine Bowen,
her 1:1 training and much much more, just go to her website:
www.winkiespiers.com

Winkie, Dennis & Maisie

SHORT STACK PUBLISHING
PRESENTS

How to Handle Living With Your Dog

By Winkie Spiers

SHORT STACK PUBLISHING

This edition published in Great Britain by Short Stack Publishing

www.shortstackpublishing.com

10 9 8 7 6 5 4 3 2 1

#4 in The How to Handle Series
Series Editor Oscar Dyson

ISBN-13: 978-1-906467-03-6

CONTENTS

PHOTOGRAPHS

This book would have been incomplete without photographs of 'real life' dogs. In this sense we mean 'real-life' in that they are not posed or in some way manipulated. Happily many dogs and their owners have very kindly given permission for their photographs to be used. The vast majority of the fabulous photographs are from Winkie's personal photographic library but those that are not given full credit below!

Dennis, Maisie & countless friends © Winkie Spiers

Ace, page 84 © Anna West

Bella, page 85 © Dirk Lottering

Cody & Winston, page 34 © Jack Haycraft

Flo, page 85 © Jessica Bauermeister

Frannie's Puppies, page 34 © Mark Sanders

Maisie, page 85 © Peter Lambert

McKenzie, page 80 © Jodi Rosluk

To Dennis

who has contributed more than he knows to
my personal and professional development

FOREWORD

It is rare to find a book that actually addresses the most important area of owning a dog: that of living with each other within a demanding society in order that all parties can co-exist peaceably. The market has been inundated with books on dog training, but these tend to focus on the superficial ideas of control and obedience. What has been needed for some time is something that continues my own teaching: tackling the more important areas such as encouraging mutual understanding and good communication skills along with decision making and coping strategies. This should also include how to bring up a dog to make sensible choices rather than only being able to act in a sensible way when told what to do.

Winkie Spiers gives an uncomplicated guide for pet dog owners that provides a wealth of sensible information. Her down-to-earth approach puts both dog and owner first, rather than focussing on the "method" that is so common amongst dog owners and trainers. The stance she takes means that we can at last begin to understand our dogs, to find out why they act as they do and not only to identify their needs but also to know how best to meet many of them.

City and country living with dogs may demand many different skills, but Winkie offers suggestions that will enable owners to help their dogs learn how to gradually cope in a variety of environments. Anyone who is really knowledgeable about dogs will understand that there is no safe "quick fix". It is clear that the best behaviour comes from a carefully prepared programme building on basic skills. Winkie understands that one of the most common mistakes is to do too much too soon, thereby pushing dogs into a position they are ill-prepared to cope with. In addition she actively promotes the Canine Bowen Technique, the results of which are achieving far-reaching consequences for dog and owner alike. In short, Winkie is keen to advocate a range of strategies designed to enhance the life quality of all dogs and their human companions.

Sheila Harper BEd, BA
Staffordshire, UK

Chapter One

"He is your friend, your partner, your defender, your dog.
You are his life, his love, his leader. He will be yours, faithful and
true, to the last beat of his heart.
You owe it to him to be worthy of such devotion."

Anon

INTRODUCTION

Why is 'How To Handle Living With Your Dog' (HTHLWYD) special?

In short it's because there are a great many books written on how to train your dog but these don't address how we *live* with our dogs. This book is a no-nonsense guide on how to live with your dog harmoniously; with mutual understanding and good communication. Living with one or more dogs should be enjoyable and if it's not then you need to learn more to improve your knowledge about them and to improve your relationship to mutual benefit. Throughout my time working with dogs and their owners both in classes and 1:1, I've identified a core group of questions that come up time and time again so I've ensured this book answers all those questions.

Who will benefit from reading HTHLWYD?

This book will be useful for anyone thinking of getting a dog or puppy, anyone having problems with a current dog, (be they a puppy, older dog, a pedigree, a Heinz 57 and/or a rescue dog). It will help you in any situation where things between you and your dog are not as happy as they could be; where there is room for improvement or where you just want to get to know and understand your dog better.

So, what *is* a dog?

Well, apparently they're man's best friend. But are we theirs?

First off, let's find out more about dogs.

Dogs are a member of the canid family, other types include wolves, foxes, wild dogs, dingos, coyotes. Out of all the types of canid, dogs are the only ones to have become truly domesticated and as such they have been living with humans for about 12,000 to 14,000 years, yet have been around and evolving for millions of years.

Eyewatering capabilities:

Since dogs became domesticated we humans have developed, through selective breeding, many different shapes and sizes of dog who perform a great variety of jobs.

The uses we find for dogs are constantly evolving as we discover just how amazing their senses and abilities are. For instance we now have dogs that can sniff out tumours, detect diabetes in urine, find drugs, weapons and land mines, not to mention the assistance dogs for the blind, deaf, epileptic, elderly and wheelchair users. We have dogs that can rescue people from water, hunt down criminals, find people who are lost in the countryside or buried under rubble, find cadavers, tow boats, retrieve game, hunt, point, herd, pull sleds, do tricks, perform in films or on stage, we experiment on them, bet on them, show them... And all this only scratches the surface: their uses seem endless and the jobs we find for them limitless.

Who knows what we might see in the future with the vast range above being only a tiny sample of what we've found for dogs to do. Have we even realised half of their capabilities? Only time will tell.

Despite their phenomenal capabilities, if our dogs step out of line we often judge them harshly. Generally if a dog growls or nips it's in big trouble yet if our pet cat hisses, spits, scratches or bites we just tell whoever is the recipient of this behaviour to leave them alone. If a horse bites or kicks it might be punished but generally we put a red ribbon on the tail of a horse that is likely to kick when out and about and we put a sign up outside the stable to advise people not to stroke or touch one that bites. The cat or horse is unlikely to lose it's life for an indiscretion but a dog is. We will often put some time and effort into making a horse or a cat more comfortable being touched but it's not always our first thought with a dog.

 We expect a lot from our dogs, and sometimes too much. It's time to redress the balance.

Different breeds of dog have very distinct drives and instincts, for example; many terriers have a strong prey drive, love to go down holes and naturally derive a great deal of pleasure from chasing small furry things...

Collies tend to have a strong herding instinct and will try to herd people, ducks, horses etc as well as sheep. Greyhounds, whippets and lurchers are built for speed and love to sprint and course things and that can include other dogs, birds, cats, rabbits, deer, runners, cyclists and even rollerbladers and skateboarders etc.

Sighthounds are generally built for speed, and not endurance.

Labradors love to swim and retrieve things and often want to carry items around in their mouths, perhaps our shoes or their toys (though often these are the same thing as far as they are concerned...)

Newfoundlands just adore water and are extremely strong swimmers, they will often try to rescue people in water and even try to tow any boats that are about!

Above: This Newfoundland had just retrieved the large log from a nearby pond. Newfoundlands are very strong and can comfortably swim surprisingly long distances.

Below: Lurchers enjoy their home comforts. They tend to have fairly thin coats, this combined with their slim build means they're not suited to lying on hard surfaces. This one finds the sofa infinitely preferable!

A dog's natural instincts can often conflict with what we want from a dog so it's important that you research a breed that has traits that you like to limit the opportunity for conflict, misunderstanding, disappointment and frustration. You should think about your lifestyle before you get a dog, and try to research a breed or mix of breeds which will enjoy and fit in to that lifestyle. For example if you love jogging, some of the larger breeds (eg Mastiff, Deerhound, Great Dane) can be unsuitable for long distance running and certainly the sight hounds (Whippets, Greyhounds, Lurchers, etc) don't always enjoy and are not physically designed for long distance running. They are better at short sprints and then some gentle ambling or sofa time. If a pristine spick and span house is top of your priorities then some of the longer haired breeds may not be ideal for you; dogs with long or thick coats need regular grooming and care and tend to leave a lot of hair around. Dogs require and deserve good and appropriate care and I think we owe it to them to learn more about them generally. It's also important to treat them like dogs and with respect.

So how does all this impact on how we live with our dogs?

The impact of us not learning enough about our dogs and thus caring for them appropriately is more often than not dissatisfaction on both sides; unhappiness and frustration for both dog and owner. Quite often we have no idea of the history of our chosen breed, and little knowledge of the history of the individual dog. If you've already got a dog, stop and think: why did you choose your particular dog? Was it looks, temperament, size, love at first sight, had one as a child?

There are a myriad of reasons why we choose our dogs but do we consider seriously enough if our lifestyle is suited to that particular type of dog? What we want from dogs is ever changing, historically they were used for working and sport and tended to live in social groups but now they often live alone (sometimes alone for long periods every day) they can be status symbols, fashion accessories or companions and we constantly change the boundaries. Our expectations change: frequently one minute we want a free running and joyful pet then perhaps an obedient one, one that enjoys a busy weekend with lots of activity followed by a week of being alone with no stimulation.

We may go to dog shows or competitions and expect them to behave appropriately with little or no preparation. We have lovely holidays and weekends with them then all of sudden it's back to work and being alone again. Dogs can now have passports and travel abroad but do we spend enough time preparing them to be able to cope with long car journeys or flights? Many dogs now live in flats without access to the outside at all and spend long periods of time without access to any toileting areas, how do we prepare them for this type of lifestyle? Living in cities and quite often in isolation for long periods can be very hard and stressful for such a social creature so by spending time preparing them and thinking about how to teach them to cope we can make all these types of situation easier for them and us. It's about having realistic expectations, preparation and being consistent.

Above all else our time with our dogs should be enjoyable for both them and us.

Chapter Two

COMMUNICATION

"I used to look at my dog and think, 'If you were a little smarter you could tell me what you were thinking,' and he'd look at me like he was saying, 'If you were a little smarter, I wouldn't have to.' "

~ *Fred Jungclaus*

How do dogs communicate?

In many ways humans and dogs differ in their style of communication which can lead to frustration, misunderstanding and problem behaviour (both for dogs and their owners!) Just think: how frustrated do we feel when someone doesn't understand or listen to us or even worse punishes us for trying to communicate? Dogs communicate with each other using all of their senses; scent & pheromones, smell, taste, touch, sight but they primarily communicate with each other and us using body language and facial expressions. On the other hand to a great extent humans tend to rely on verbal skills, and often far too much!

Canine communication is essential for learning, reproduction and hunting. From the first moment we are with our dogs they are watching us and reading our body language, we often chatter away to them but what they are most interested in is what our bodies are telling them. Body language doesn't lie!

Skills that aren't to be sniffed at?

Scent plays a large part in communication in dogs but it's something that we can't really learn to be a part of; it's not really our forte. But we can observe it in the way that they smell where other dogs or species have been and how they leave scent markers behind for others. If you are interested in developing deeper knowledge on this are specifically see the recommended reading and information sources on pages 104 & 105.

A classic misinterpretation:

"My dog knows when he's done something wrong, you can see it!"
No! He knows that you're cross. And that is not the same thing at all!
When someone tells me their dog knows when it's done something wrong I have to disagree. All the dog knows is that your body is tense and that you're angry, and that it's not in their interests or desirable. Thus they use appeasing gestures to calm us down. This is often misinterpreted as guilt.

Dogs live in the now (ideally where we should spend more time but that's a whole other matter!). They rarely connect something they did in the past (great examples being chewing up your leather sofa, or soiling your new rug) with your arguably understandable explosive and negative responses and reactions. To be clear: for a dog the 'past' can be 5 minutes, 5 hours or 5 days ago. With anger, and expressions of that anger, all we are teaching them is that we are unpredictable and not particularly nice. They feel we are exhibiting aggressive behaviour to them for no fathomable reason. The next time you are angry or irritated they will re-double their efforts to appease and be nice. Worse than that though, in extreme and repeated cases dogs will just shut down and accept what's going on; believing there is nothing that they can do to influence the outcome.

Learning to be tidy with your own possessions and create a dog friendly environment is one simple but exceptionally effective (not to mention less stressful) way to go. For example: a client once asked what they could do to stop their dog stealing things from their handbag when it was on the floor. The solution was pretty easy: don't leave your handbag on the floor! Just hang your handbag up out of the dog's way.

Body language

People use body language pretty much all the time to communicate but often don't realise let alone acknowledge the role that body language plays in our lives or notice the impact that it has on our dogs or of course on other people. Dogs have a greater critical distance than we do: even dogs that know each other really well rarely want to be very close to each other all the time. Dogs need space; whereas we are happy to walk closely or arm in arm with someone we are fond of, though of course we're not happy if a stranger invades our space.

We humans also use touch a lot more than dogs do: we don't often see them stroking, cuddling or touching each other. That's not to say that they don't like what we do but it's important to remember to respect their natural way of behaving. We usually prefer closeness with people who we know and trust, a stranger coming up and putting their arm around you would not be very welcome (and would in fact be rather forward to say the least!) but a friend or family member would be fine. Dogs are the same and will enjoy or tolerate touching and cuddling from someone they know more readily than strangers, thus respect and common sense should be employed.

Recently at a meeting I thought carefully about human body language and was put in a position where I could practice some and observe the reaction. I sat next to a man who I didn't know and I didn't enjoy his body language at all as he put his arm along the back of my seat making me most uncomfortable by invading my space. I wondered how using my body language I could get him to change what he was doing. (I was listening to a speaker so asking verbally was not really an option. Elbowing or kicking was momentarily tempting, but again, not really appropriate.) I tried glancing back at the offending arm but he merely smiled at me, I then fidgeted to no avail and finally I slightly moved my chair and moved myself further back in the seat and sat up straighter using the back of the chair and he finally moved his arm. We do things like this daily but do we always think about what we're doing or why.

 Do we notice when our dogs are uncomfortable with what we're doing?

Turid Rugaas is a wonderfully knowledgeable Norwegian lady who has studied dog behaviour and how they communicate with each other for over 30 years. She calls what they do 'Calming Signals' as they use their body language and social skills to communicate peaceful intention, avoid conflict or threats and to calm themselves and others down in stressful, fearful, unpleasant, excited or noisy situations. Turid discovered that by observing the signals that dogs use with each other we can increase our ability to understand and communicate with our dogs. In a similar vein wolf expert, David Mech, noticed wolves communicate with physical signals and he refers to what they do as 'cut off signals'. So how can we use this information?

Dogs that are kept in isolation for long periods can lose the ability to use these signals but they can mostly be regained to some extent. A well socialised dog will be well versed in communication and interestingly it's a universal language that dogs worldwide understand and use. You may even see other species such as cats using their body language to communicate with a dog. It's not really that different to the way we can lose our social skills if we don't practice them. If we don't meet new people very often we will feel stressed and anxious when we do; lacking in confidence and feeling tongue tied and perhaps even behaving inappropriately.

Don't panic you don't need to be Turid Rugas, David Mech or Sherlock Holmes to understand your dog, and pick up on the clues. But you do need to have a basic grasp of just what signals and clues you should be looking out for when observing and interacting with your dog.

"Lots of people talk to animals," said Pooh. "Not that many listen though. That's the problem."' Benjamin Hoff, The Tao of Pooh

Key 'Clues'

Head turning: can be a tiny or large movement, a swift or slow movement, can be held for some time or done several times quickly: many variations of this one move can be seen in different circumstances.

Above: the terrier (on the right) is turning his head away from both the camera and the other dog and the deerhound has his eyes averted so whilst his head is facing the camera his eyes are looking away

Commonly dogs turn their heads away when we take a photograph of them as the directness of our look and pointing a camera at them makes them politely turn their heads away.   I had many pictures of dogs turning away from the camera and it was only by going on some of Turid's courses that I was able to understand why they would rarely gaze into the camera for that cute picture that I was trying for.

Direct eye contact between dogs is impolite and at worst hostile, it's the same with people but we don't often think about it. Staring directly at a dog will make it feel very uncomfortable, they can learn to look at us but it's not a natural or polite thing for them to spend time looking directly at us or other dogs. We may feel uneasy or suspicious if someone stares directly at us and use our own body language to try to deflect the gaze. When taking photos very often people turn away when the camera is focused on them, we learn to look into the camera when someone wants to snap us but it's not always the natural or comfortable thing to do.

The most common time when staring intently into another's eyes is OK in human terms is when we're being gooey looking at someone we love! More normally we will use head turning or glancing away to keep eye contact in within polite boundaries.

Different breeds of dog will find it harder to use some signals, for instance the dogs which are bred with shortened noses; Boxer, Bulldog, Pug etc won't have the same outline of face so it might be harder for other dogs to understand their head turns or dips. Very hairy dogs will have difficulty using their eyes and head dips. We can use head turning to great effect if we don't want attention from a dog, this will be touched upon again later in this book.

Clearly turning away from the camera & photographer

Head dipping: like head turning, head dipping can be done in different ways, watch two sensible dogs see each other on the park and you may notice a head dip followed by a head turn or a sniff on the ground. They are aware of each other and glance in the direction of the other dog but do some very subtle moves using head dipping and turning; once you start watching and seeing it's hard to stop. Again in some breeds the head dip may not be so obvious.

This Hungarian Pulli is covered in dreadlocks from head to toe and any subtle moves may well be missed by us and other dogs. Due to its thick coat this type of breed will struggle to make any head dips, head turns, eye contact or lip licking very obvious.

Lip licking: this can be seen well on a short haired black dogs but hairy breeds will have difficulty with this signal being seen as their hair my obscure their tongue. This is often a quick lick of the nose or lips and can be so quick that we barely see it, other times it's a slower signal that we don't have any problem seeing.

At the vet's you may notice an increase in lip licking, when you pick a dog up it might lick lip more. Watch your dog and other people's dogs to see when they use this signal and try to interpret why. You need to spend time learning the nuances of your own dog's behaviour, you cannot hope for a broad brush interpretation.

This dog is lip licking as the camera and human are too close and being quite direct.

With this type of breed we can see a lip lick very clearly.

Blinking: use of the eyes in looking away, blinking a lot or slowly, half closing the eyes, hard eyes, soft eyes... Eyes can be very expressive (we use our eyes a lot; think about how you use your eyes with your dog and with other people). Dogs use their eyes to soften what they are saying much as we do, you may see a dog growl at another dog if it tries to approach a toy but the eyes will quickly soften and look away as they are saying 'that's mine' but keeping it polite and not wanting any hostility or conflict. If a dog doesn't actually turn its head away from a direct look it may just glance away, we can use our eyes to signal our peaceful and loving intentions towards our dogs.

Ear position: the ears can tell us and other dogs a lot with some quick changes of position, these may include flattening the ears, pricking the ears and moving them rapidly or slowly (obviously something very few of us can do!!) It's worth watching and understanding what your dog might be feeling and thinking with different ear positions as it will give you a clue as to what's going on. Remember that a dog's hearing can be up to four times better than ours so in some circumstances they may be pricking their ears and reacting to things that we can't even hear.

Freezing/staying very still: this may occur in the stand, sit or down position. You may see your dog stand very still if unsure of something, or perhaps if you speak harshly or loudly or if it feels threatened by another dog.

Above: the terrier is not comfortable with the dalmation so he is standing very still, looking away and turning his head, his stance is upright and not inviting the other dog to come closer

Sometimes staying very still can be in invitation to a less confident dog to approach or just a moment for them to assess a situation. It's important to look at the whole situation as sometimes freezing and staying very still can be because the dog is frightened or worried.   In working dogs such as pointers we see freezing or 'pointing' when they indicate where a bird is so again this signal can have many interpretations.

Walking or moving slowly: these slow (or slowing) movements can be done when standing, sitting or lying down. They can be a way of approaching politely or trying to defuse a situation. Sometimes if an owner recalls their dog rather sharply or loudly, or if their body posture is perceived as being hostile the dog will slow down as it approaches and may curve (see page 23) as well, as it attempts to calm the situation down. Also bear in mind that walking or moving slowly if it's unusual for your dog may be an indication that it's not feeling well or experiencing some pain so always speak to your vet if in any doubt.

Yawning: a clear one for us to see and use. Yawns may come in quick succession, and whilst they may be quiet they often make a (sometimes somewhat comical) noise as well. We often see dogs yawn when we stroke them too much or too quickly, perhaps when we pick them up. It can be a way of them trying to calming us down or sometimes calming themselves.

Rude and intrusive camera: the border terrier reacts to the camera being a little too close and looking directly at him. He regards this as (arguably only slightly) rude by stopping chewing and yawning. (Once the space was increased he went back to enjoying his chew.)

Yawning can be a way of them trying to calming us down or sometimes calming themselves. I have a dog who does noisy yawns in the car on the way to a favourite park, he could be calming himself down as he gets more excited or perhaps he just needs to control the amount of oxygen he's taking into his lungs? There are many reasons for all their signals and it's for us to get to know and observe our dogs to enable us to try and interpret what's going on.

Yawning is a great one for us to use, when things are too excited or stressful you can yawn at your dog to help calm things (do try this - the results are amazing). It's such a simple action, yet will frequently find your dog responds to you, and 'echos' or 'catches' the yawn. You may even find yourself 'catching' your dog's yawns!

Sitting down: of course dogs choose to sit down (or lie down) for all sorts of reasons. For further clues as to why they are sitting down, you really look at the whole picture, including other behaviours: the dog will still use other signals such as head turning, lip licking, turning away, moving slowly, eye movements and tail wagging. You may notice an older dog sit down when approached by a more excitable or nervous dog. In this situation it can be an invitation to interact, it can be be a way to calm the other one down or conversely to give it confidence, or it can be a way of saying 'Look, I'm not really interested'. From the human side of the equation we can use crouching or sitting down to appear less threatening to a nervous or fearful dog, or simply to be more inviting to an approaching dog or to our dogs when we are recalling them.

Lying down: usually a very non threatening gesture.

Left: this black dog is lying down very low to the ground. She felt uncomfortable with the large lurcher and was making sure that nothing got too exciting or dangerous for her. She was clearly saying 'I'm no threat to you, leave me alone'

Lying down can be a strong calming signal when used with other dogs. Again watch for head turning, head dipping, ear and tail movement, eye contact and body stance when they are lying down in order to understand more. Very commonly dogs lie down when they see another dog. Adolescent dogs sometimes do this before pouncing but older dogs will use it with younger ones, often as a friendly and open gesture. It can also be quite a submissive *'please be nice to me'* position dropped into by less confident or cautious dogs. And it can be a very strong calming signal used by a dog if approached or threatened by another dog they perceive to be dangerous.

Right: the black dog isn't particularly comfortable with the extremely direct approach of the large adolescent, so is lying down in a submissive type gesture and hoping that the big rude brute will just go away.

 If ever you have trouble with a recall just lie on the ground and see what happens!

Play position/play bow: this move can be an invitation to play but can also be to put another dog at ease or when he meets another type of animal he's not sure about. Often if we go into a play bow the dog will respond with a play bow; it's a well understood sign of happy intent to play. However of course it is not *always* the case. I have also observed dogs using the play bow when they have abdominal discomfort or aches and of course it is commonly used in the morning to stretch themselves after a good night's sleep. Anyone who has practiced yoga will know how lovely the 'down dog' position feels as it stretches many essential areas.

Left: use of play bow and lying down in an invitation to play, both dogs appear happy and comfortable with the interaction.

Curving: this we observe commonly when meeting another dog or even another type of animal.

Most well socialised adult dogs will curve when approaching another dog and come in to meet each other nose to flank. Curving is also used when a dog sees something it is in someway unsure of. Predictably with curving you will see many of the other signals used in combination.

Above: this collie has a high tail as she doesn't want the adolescent Irish Terrier to come too close. Her body is curved and her eyes are soft. There are many signals; all polite but firm and clearly telling the terrier to respect her space

Above: full on approach, and curving

When out with your dog and you find yourself approaching another dog head on, it's polite to curve away as you pass. Dogs feel a lot more comfortable if you make an effort to do this, especially on a narrow pathway.

We can use curving to great effect when putting the lead on or approaching a dog, many other species also prefer the less direct approach (including many humans!).

Curving: this terrier is curving as she walks towards the house. The lamb is in her way and staring directly at her, thus she's using curving, looking away, and moving slowly with a low tail carriage (amongst other signals) to avoid a 'lamb head butting' or any other unwanted encounter.

Displacement activity: this is something that a dog may do when it feels uncomfortable, anxious, over-excited or bored and doesn't know what else to do e.g. sniffing, urinating, picking up a toy, chewing sticks, excessive licking. When this happens it's good idea to think about what is causing the behaviour and move on or calm things down. Sometimes the displacement activity stops quite quickly and sometimes it will carry on.

As humans we use displacement activities such as playing with our hair or fiddling with pens, or simply faffing about when we don't feel too comfortable in a situation. One of my dogs will dig a small hole in the grass if I stop and talk to someone for too long. He's telling me that either he's bored or finding it difficult in some way, so sometimes it's better to keep moving or give the dog something to do (something that's less destructive to the grass!).

Tail wagging: some say a dog can express more with his tail in seconds, than his owner expresses with his tongue in many hours! Although contrary to popular belief a wagging tail doesn't always mean a happy dog.

Tails wag in different ways and mean many different things, round and round or side to side, quivering in a high or low position, wagging with the whole dog moving or a slow movement from side to side, there are many variations and all will mean different things in different dogs. A high tail may mean high arousal, excitement or uncertainty and side to side may mean 'please be nice to me'.

The tail movement varies hugely from dog to dog and is obviously dependent on the type of tail and length etc. Obviously some dogs don't have a tail but you can still tell a lot from movement of the stump! Tail wagging clearly isn't something that we can do as humans but observing how dogs use their tails can provide us with a lot of information.

Tail wagging: the golden Labrador is standing still with a tail that's straight out in line with his body and his head dipped. The black and tan crossbreed dog has a high tail and is showing more interest in the Labrador than is (quite frankly) polite. However using his tail position and dipped, slightly turned head the Labrador is keeping the encounter calm and polite.

Mimicking: something that we may find ourselves doing with people we are close to, like or admire. Have you ever found yourself mimicking the body language of a friend when you are chatting? Mimicking is also a way that the young (and sometimes old!) of any species learn. We pick up mannerisms from people all the time whether we realise it or not and dogs do the same. A common thing for dogs to do when they want to calm down an excited encounter, or simply to stop play is to sniff. Indeed often when one dog breaks away from playing with another dog and starts sniffing, the other dog follows.

Mimicking behaviour AND play bowing!

Of course dogs can learn things that we don't want them to learn from other dogs. For example if you enjoy walking with a friend whose dog chases ducks, you may well find that given the opportunity your dog will start to chase ducks as well which is not an ideal thing to do in the local park. And, sadly, they can also learn bullying tactics, barking, chasing, digging, over excitement and all manner of other things so watch out!

However on the other hand, the good news is that if we (that is us and our dogs) hang out with the well behaved and well socialized adult dogs, your dog can learn good behaviours, and positive lessons too!

Mimicking: the terrier is in water with a younger dog, the lurcher (on the right). The lurcher is having her first experience of going into water. She is imitating his paddling and digging as she is unsure of what else to do. This good first experience exploring water, leads to a dog who is confident around water.

Splitting: splitting is something that an older dog may do to stop puppies or adolescents from playing too madly or to prevent an encounter from becoming difficult or stressful. Quite often young dogs (like young people) don't know when to stop and play can start to get out of hand and then damage and accidents can occur.

Right: the two puppies on the right of the picture are playing tug and the adult dog (on the left of the picture) is watching on the sidelines in case things get a little heated and the play needs to be stopped.

In the park you may well have observed two dogs playing and a third dog either trying to run between them or bark to stop them. Splitting is often interpreted as ruining a good game but dogs know better than we do when something is going too far; so it's good to listen to them. In human terms, when two children start to play a little too excitedly or roughly we distract them and encourage them to calm down before someone gets hurt. This is a technique we need to employ with our dogs as well. We can split a situation up very easily by walking between two dogs or distracting them: and trust me it's much easier to do this effectively and swiftly if we stop things before they go too far. Once play has gone on for too long, a threshold is crossed, and dogs are no longer in a position to hear or stop.

Splitting is important not only where two or more dogs are involved but also when we use our bodies to split and provide a barrier between the dog something that the dog is nervous or anxious about. Sometimes dogs try to get between human encounters and this is usually to prevent us getting too close or too excited and hurting each other.

HELP !
Communication Problems and Solutions

Examples of problem solving using better understanding of canine communication

🐾 Why does my dog not come directly to me when I call?

Sometimes this can be because our body language, stance or verbal command is perceived as threatening or aggressive by the dog so it will curve as it approaches or stop at a distance away and freeze, sit or lie down and may lick lips, yawn and turn away.

To deal with this use a gentler, happier way to call the dog verbally and change your body position to either sideways on, crouch down, sit or lie down or move away from the dog making yourself more appealing.

If the dog is in an encounter with another dog it may not come back immediately in case the other dog considers them rude, dogs need to finish their peaceful social encounter with another dog first before coming back to you to avoid any potential misunderstanding.

When sniffing the dog may not hear you if it is really concentrating on a smell, when we concentrate really hard we don't always hear others so it's nicer to give the dog the benefit of the doubt and make sure he has heard you. The dog also needs to fully understand what you mean when you call them so taking the time to train a happy recall is essential.

🐾 My dog sometimes backs away or hides behind me when someone tries to stroke him.

Many people like dogs and want to try to touch them too quickly in a head on approach with full eye contact that can make the dog feel uncomfortable.

Slowing down the approach and doing as dogs do and approaching slowly from the side can help. The ideal is to give the dog the choice; let them decide whether or not they want to meet or be introduced to the other party. Bear in mind that some days we don't feel very sociable and our dogs have days like that too; and they may not always want to be touched. Though of course you should consider also any physical problems, stress or pain when a dog doesn't like to be touched and if in doubt see your vet.

Dogs will also use us as a barrier if they can; putting us between them and something that they may be frightened or unsure of. This is a trusting thing to do and we need to listen to what our dogs are trying to tell us. If a dog shies away from another dog there is probably a good reason and we should never force unwanted meetings between our dogs and other people or animals.

🐾 When I ask my dog to sit he ignores me.

This can be because our body language is not good in dog terms or because we are standing over the dog in an intimidating way, maybe they just don't like the way we are asking and are freezing and staying very still to calm us down. Always consider the impact that our tone of voice and body language has on the dog and be sure that if you teach the sit you do it in an easy to understand way.

"Oh gosh! Were you talking to me?"

Dogs never want to anger us or have conflict; so think about why they might not be doing as asked and consider the possible explanations. Perhaps they are physically not comfortable to do as you ask, or perhaps they are confused about what you are asking them to do, or perhaps the surface you are asking them to sit on is not ideal, perhaps too slippery, too hard, too cold, too hot. Recently I took my shoes off on a hot day and the paving slabs were far too hot for me to walk on comfortably. Think about the whole situation and in the case of surface temperatures do bear in mind that tarmac and pavements get very hot and can be horridly uncomfortable for a dog.

Another flooring issue arises from the increasing prevalance of laminate flooring. Although popular and practical in many ways, these floors can be very slippery for dogs and make for a difficult surface to do anything on which can lead to physical aches, problems and pain.

Sometimes we can also ask too much of our dogs and they could be too tired, too over-stimulated, the training has gone on for too long or perhaps just not in the mood! Always think about why the dog doesn't want to do something and never force them.

My dog keeps jumping up at people.

Dogs often learn to jump up because they get rewarded for it. Puppies are often encouraged to jump up, as when they do so people touch them and talk to them which is rewarding and nice. Then when they get older and bigger all of a sudden the humans get cross about jumping up and the dogs end up being confused.

When a dog jumps up the easy way for them to understand that we don't want to be jumped on is to turn away as that's what they usually do with each other.   Remember dogs stay still, move slowly and turn their heads and bodies away from other dogs when they don't like something, so they are familiar with what such actions mean. By being consistent and teaching our friends to use the same technique we can change this unwanted behaviour in a nice and easy to understand way.

Simply saying 'off', 'get down' and 'no' can all be confusing as the dog often has no idea of what all our different words mean. They can even misinterpret them as rewarding remarks as we engaging with them and talking to them.   Similarly we often touch the dog as we push them off, this can be unpleasant for the dog, but can also be interpreted as us liking what they are doing (they may feel you are using touch to show affection and approval). Ironically in some situations they may feel they are even helping us: believing they are splitting us from unwanted situations and inertaction or simply trying to calm us down.

The best way to deal jumping up in most situations is to keep quiet, be calm and initially turn your head away and if that doesn't work turn your whole body away. But (as should be clear by now) it's terribly important to look at why the dog is jumping up. Is there a pattern? Does the dog jump up more when it's confused? When it's had too much exercise? When it's over-tired? When it's overexcited?   Dealing with the cause or root of the problem, is the most effective way of identifying a long term solution.

SIGNALS WE CAN USE

To recap here are some examples of signals we can use with our dogs

Slowing down and curving when approaching any dog especially one that is over-stimulated, excited, nervous, fearful, stressed, or anxious.

Yawning when the dog is having trouble calming down or settling.

Sitting or crouching down when touching a dog rather than standing over it and try to avoid putting your arm over the back of the dog, perhaps just touch the side closest to you.

🐾 Turning away with body or just the head when approaching, or being approached by dogs

🐾 Splitting,　going in between two dogs that are getting over excited, splitting to break hard eye contact or just put yourself between your dog and another dog when passing on a narrow path.

🐾 Moving calmly, quietly and slowly.

🐾 Being polite to your dog and understanding what it is that they're trying to tell us usually helps to build a trusting and harmonious relationship.

How to Tell When A Dog is Starting to Feel Uncomfortable:

When you see your dog using it's body language and the signals are becoming more frequent and stronger it will be time to do something. A dog that is consistently ignored when it's trying to tell you something will start to speak a little 'louder'. So for example whilst your dog may have started by head turning, yawning and lip licking; when no-one notices it may move onto panting, whining, chewing, barking, being silly, scratching, biting at the lead or any other displacement activities.

Ideally we notice our dogs' signals early on and we remove the dog or the problem from the situation. But if the dog is still being ignored or worse being told off it may move onto growling. Of course quite often growling is punished but it's often the only way that a dog can get our attention when all other ways of letting us know that they are not coping very well have failed. Growling is also our real warning signal so that we know that the dog is really not coping if we've ignored everything else and at this point we should take the dog immediately out of the situation.

If a growl fails to get a response the dog might really shout and in desperation to be listened to, may even nip. This is not what we want at all and a dog that is never listened to might learn that nipping is the only way to get noticed, unchecked this may lead to biting. And in a worst case scenario biting may lead to a dog being destroyed.

Think about how we deal with each other and if we are consistently ignored we will talk more loudly, that doesn't work so we might shout, shouting doesn't work so there could be door slamming, pushing, lashing out, hitting. Bad communication or lack of communication may lead to a lot of stress, much frustration and unhappiness. Growling is often our early warning system and should not be punished, you should be looking at the cause.

USEFUL STRATEGIES TO HELP YOUR DOG OUT

🐾• Learn more about how dogs communicate, there are a few good books on the subject (see pages 104 & 105).

🐾 Observe and listen to your dog, find out its likes and dislikes. Wherever possible give your dog choices.

🐾 Don't force confrontation with other dogs or people. Again, give your dog choices.

🐾 Try not to use a loud, harsh or irritable voice.

🐾 Teach children how to approach dogs calmly and quietly and always get them to ask the owner or handler if it's OK before approaching any dog.

🐾 If your dog is prone to get excited, growl, bark or lunge at other dogs when on a lead give it more space, curve around the other dogs or elect to move further away.

🐾 Watch for your dog's reaction to other dogs, people and situations and if in doubt move away keeping yourself between the dog and whatever is making it feel uneasy.

🐾 Allow your dogs to practice their social skills regularly with other 'good' or 'nice' dogs.

🐾 When your dog is stressed or over-excited get it out of the situation, sit down somewhere peaceful. You could try yawning at the dog.

🐾🐾 Watch your dog and other dogs in their interactions and try to understand what's going on and what they are saying. Just think how frustrating it must be for them to try to tell us things when we just don't listen!

Obviously you're not going to turn in Dr Dolittle overnight. But by keeping a close eye on your dog's body language and becoming more concious of your own you'll understand your dog much much better, and you'll help him to understand you.

Chapter Three

THE STAGES OF A DOG'S LIFE
PUPPIES ~ ADOLESCENTS ~ ADULTS

"Even the biggest dog has been a pup."
~ Joaquin Miller

STAGE 1: PUPPYHOOD
(0 - 6 months)

🐾 How do you select the right dog for you?

Why are you attracted to a particular breed? Is it a breed that is suited to your lifestyle? Many people choose a dog based on what it looks like without considering the traits, instincts, exercise, lifestyle and care required. The internet has loads of information about different breeds, the Kennel Club website (www.thekennelclub.org.uk) has plenty of useful information on a great many breeds and most breeds have their own clubs where you can find out even more about the type of dog you are considering.

Many trainers and behaviourists offer pre-puppy consultations to help you to choose a dog that's right for you and it's worth taking the time and effort to find out as much as possible about your chosen breed or type as many dogs live for well over 10 years.

🐾 How should you prepare your home for a puppy?

Think about where your puppy is going sleep, which areas of the house it's going to be allowed into and how you can make an area safe for the puppy. This will mean you won't need to worry about it chewing electric cables, shoes, furniture or soiling the carpet when you're not around. Do you want to use a crate for the puppy to sleep in? Will it live in the kitchen or another room? Is the garden or outside area safe and suitable for a puppy, can it escape or eat anything poisonous?

There are so many things to think about and there are many, many books with lots of advice on different ways to care for your puppy. Bear in mind that it's all individual and being consistent and having a suitable routine is the key, whatever you decide to do. Will you need to arrange puppy care for times when you're not at home? Does everyone in your household want a puppy? Do you need to prepare any other household pets for the arrival of a puppy? With pre-planning and thought the arrival of a puppy into your home can be great fun for all concerned.

There needs to be an area where the puppy has its food and where the water bowl is easily accessible all the time. The puppy needs its own bed, at least one: but ideally somewhere to call it's own in each room where it might spend time. You need suitable toys, chews and treats for your puppy as well as food. In the beginning you will probably keep the puppy on the same food provided by the breeder but you might want to speak to someone at your vet who is qualified or knowledgeable about nutrition as early good and appropriate nutrition is very important for the puppy's growth and development and different breeds may have different nutritional requirements so do some research and speak to qualified professionals.

Make your home as puppy friendly as possible and remove the possibility for him to chew anything that's not his or anything unsuitable, dangerous or precious to you. Learn to be tidy! When owners complain that their puppies have chewed shoes, pens, books, clothing, handbags etc (as touched upon earlier) I have to ask why the

puppy had access to these items in the first place! Leaving your things lying around is inviting problems as puppies (and older dogs) are naturally inquisitive, just as we take care to avoid our possessions being stolen we should also make sure that the puppy doesn't have temptation left around. When something does get destroyed then in my experience, in the vast majority of cases, I've found it to be the fault of the owner and not the puppy. Remember they are young and learning about the world so they need to be taught with tolerance, patience, knowledge and common sense. Ensure that your puppy has a variety of chews and toys available at all times and rotate the toys to keep them interesting. You will then minimise the interest in things that aren't theirs.

🐾 Early days with a puppy: what to expect & how to handle it

Puppies respond well to a clear and consistent approach with a feeding and toileting routine that is suitable for the age and breed. In the first 8 weeks of life puppies don't have enough knowledge to learn to avoid dangerous situations and won't learn from any negative experiences so it's important to keep the puppy safe and only use kind and up-to-date training methods: punishment of any kind is undesirable and should be avoided. Puppies need to be allowed to explore as this helps their decision making skills and helps them to learn independence. So a puppy friendly area where they can't get into any trouble or danger is important. The puppy will require plenty of sleep along with sensible exercise and opportunities to explore and socialise.

The first few nights in a new home may be frightening and will probably be the first time that the puppy has been alone and parted from it's mother and siblings so think about how you are going to deal with this in a kind and practical way that the puppy is able to understand. Puppies who are slightly older, (by which I mean over 10 weeks) when they go to their new homes, seem to cope a lot better.

🐾 Puppy Classes & Puppy Parties

It's important for puppies to meet other dogs and learn to socialise, it's good for them to meet different breeds and sizes of other dogs and older dogs as well as other puppies. Think about what your puppy is learning in a puppy class, ideally there won't be too many dogs in the class so that it's not too overwhelming for them. Ideally they'll meet in a safe and appropriate way without too much excitement, noise and unsupervised play.

Play is important for puppies to learn instinctive behaviour but without supervision they will just get over-excited and their expectation will be to play every time they meet another dog which is not ideal. Walking and socialising with older well socialised dogs is good as other dogs are better able to teach them how to behave appropriately than we are. As humans grow up we are taught that it's not desirable to continue rolling around on the floor playing into our teenage years let alone into our twenties but for some reason dogs playing constantly seems to indulge many owners. But owners need to remember that it's not normal adult dog behaviour and can lead to bullying, injuries, aggression and behaviour problems.

When I run puppy classes I restrict the numbers of puppies to three or four per class so that each owner gets plenty of individual attention and the puppy is not overwhelmed by too many other puppies. If there are too many dogs it is very distracting and the puppy will find it difficult to learn.

Calm & comfortable in a confined space

Many puppies have a few weeks during the vaccination period where they don't meet any other dogs. If their first experience with other dogs is then a large and noisy class where they get very over-excited, this doesn't make for a good first impression. Don't rush into formal training immediately; learning to cope in a variety of situations is more important than learning to sit, down and stay. Dogs can learn obedience at any time but I consider coping skills to be most important.

Take the time to find a class where the teachers are happy for you to come along and observe without your puppy. Check that the teachers are appropriately trained in up-to-date methods, check that they're insured and that they're (ideally) a member of a professional organisation where they commit to annually improve their skills and continue to learn.

Puppies should not go running or jogging with you or do any jumping or forced activity until they are fully grown. There is potential for long term physical damage and it may affect growth, and will certainly affect behaviour.

🐾 Why does my puppy bite me and everything else?

Puppies use their mouths to explore new textures, tastes and what something is: it's their way of finding out about the

world. Human babies seem to go through a phase of putting everything in their mouths and it is in fact a normal and common developmental stage in many species.

Your puppy may also experience teething pain just like babies do and biting may be a way of easing the pain and encouraging the baby teeth to fall out making room for the adult teeth.

Puppies love to explore different textures and tastes

Normally puppies start to lose their baby teeth at around 20 weeks, you may notice an increase in intensity and frequency of biting around this time or even some blood coming from their teeth or gums. If you have any concerns don't hesitate to pop into your vet for advice from the vet or the veterinary nurse.

Biting is a normal and essential part of puppy development, they need to learn what their teeth do to continue to learn bite inhibition as they get older. The intensity of bite will vary depending on the breed, experiences and individual personality of the dog.   From observation in puppy classes I have noticed that puppies who stay with their mothers and siblings until at least 10 weeks bite less than ones re-homed earlier.

How can I deal with the biting?

Firstly look at the puppy's environment: does the puppy have enough suitable toys and chews to keep him busy? Does he have enough appropriate mental stimulation? (Note: see Chapter 6, page 80, on Mental Stimulation and Games for more ideas.) Does he have right sort of exercise or perhaps too much exercise? Sleep is very important for puppies, lack of sleep or too much stimulation may result in hyperactive or destructive tendencies and increased biting. Set out below are some factors that can increase the biting problem:

- Rough or unsupervised games with members of the household, friends or other dogs or puppies
- Teething: painful or sore gums
- Too much excitement or over stimulation
- Attention for biting: it's possible that our response to biting can be stimulating to the puppy!

🐾 Not enough sleep or calm time

🐾 Unsupervised access to children: never leave dogs and children together unsupervised

🐾 Physical punishment

🐾 Teasing

🐾 People speaking in a high voice and waving arms about

🐾 Too much or too little exercise

🐾 Boredom: not enough constructive attention or stimulation

Punishment can make the biting worse; bright and reactive puppies may bite more and harder in retaliation, sensitive pups can become fearful, stoic puppies may become withdrawn, insecure puppies may become bullies and demanding puppies will bite more to get the attention. There is also the fear that the puppy doesn't understand what you're punishing it for and it will therefore become fearful and untrusting of you. Punishment should never be used.

He bites = You "YELP !" When the puppy bites you: 'yelp' out loud and stop what you were doing, perhaps turn your back to the puppy or remove yourself from the room or situation. Yelping is what another puppy or dog would do if bitten, so dogs generally understand what is meant when we do it. In all cases be calm and consistent.

🐾 What sort of things can I give my puppy to do?

Kongs: these are on sale in most pet shops and some vet surgeries and can be filled with a variety of things that the puppy likes and can keep them occupied for sometime. Most Kongs come with suggestions and ideas on how to fill and use them, and they come in many shapes and sizes. Plenty more information and ideas on sizes and fillings can be found on their website (www.kongcompany.com)

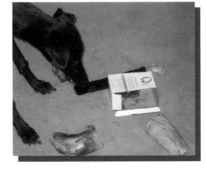

Boxes: any old and empty cardboard boxes (cereal, light bulb, egg etc) can have a few treats or bits of dried food put in them and the puppy has to find way to get the food out. If they chew up the cardboard it's not usually a problem: it doesn't usually taste good enough to eat but the challenge can provide fun and amusement for the puppy.

Hide and seek: hiding a few treats or dry food around the house or garden can stimulate them to use their noses and search them out This can provide entertainment for them, along with mental stimulation, and it's great fun to watch and observe your puppy's nascent skills developing.

Scatter feeding: if your puppy eats dry food it's sometimes fun to scatter it around on the floor or in a clean area of the garden for them. This slows down eating and makes mealtimes last that little bit longer.

The above list offers just a few ideas but there are a lot of other things that I'm sure you can think of. See pages 104 & 105 for a reading list which includes a good book of games to play with your dog.

PUPPY PROBLEMS & SOLUTIONS

🐾 **Sick in the car?** Quite often the first experience the puppy has of a car is when it is taken away from its mum and siblings, which can be quite a frightening experience. Make sure before you collect the puppy that you have plenty of paper towels and cloths to hand in case they're sick. And keep calm if it happens. You will also need to have water with you for the puppy. It makes it easier for the puppy if it has some company on the drive so having someone sitting close to the puppy or with the puppy on their knee can help it to feel reassured. Always remember that first impressions are often lasting impressions so endeavour to make that first journey as enjoyable as possible.

🐾 **House-training**: one of the first things that owners want to teach the puppy is where to toilet. The calmer and happier the puppy is the less accidents you will have. Whatever you are using, newspaper, litter box, puppy pads, garden, balcony... whatever: be consistent and reward verbally and sometimes with a food reward for going in the right place.

Completely ignore it when they go in the wrong place and whatever you do don't punish your dog for an accident as this will create anxiety, unhappiness and potentially more accidents.

When they wake up and after meals take them to the toileting area and stay with them until they have gone. Don't try to rush house-training and be calm. When you visit with friends or allow your puppy into new areas of your home do it on-lead so that the puppy doesn't get over excited and run around and have an accident. If we did nothing there is a good chance that the dog would house-train itself as they don't like to foul in their bed area and slowly your whole home will become their home/bed area and therefore they will want to toilet away from it.

If accidents happen they are usually in an area that the dog doesn't normally have access to for example the spare room. One of my own dogs prefers not to even use the garden and waits for his walks so that he can relieve himself away from his home. If you have problems speak to your vet in case there is a physical reason or find a good trainer in your area.

🐾 **Crying at night**: many puppies are unhappy for the first few nights if they have to sleep alone. It's perfectly normal as it's often the first time that they've been away from their mothers, and then on top of that it's the first time that they've been alone so it's pretty understandable.   Think before you get your puppy: how you are going to deal with potential broken/sleepless nights? Do you want to consult a dog trainer

This puppy is happy in the crate with lots of things to do

prior to getting the puppy about planning where you want the puppy to sleep and the methods you are going to use? Crate training is popular for many owners but look at all the options and choose one that suits you and your puppy, being consistent is extremely important. There are many, many options which are kind and sensible so explore all the options; there is never just one way to do things and it's very important that you feel comfortable with whatever method you choose to handle this problem.

🐾 **Grooming**: many breeds need grooming on a regular basis so it's good to start from early on but in as gentle a way as possible. Bear in mind that puppy skin is particularly sensitive and choose soft brushes to start with and do a little bit of grooming when they are relaxed and try to build it up slowly. Watch their signals and if they are yawning and turning their head away a lot or trying to get away give them a break: with time and patience they can learn to enjoy being groomed. Try to avoid using force and when choosing a professional groomer for your dog go and observe them working with other dogs first to see if you like the way that they handle the dogs.

🐾 **Beds**: What bed? Where to put it? Choose a bed that is suitable for your breed and type of dog. Hairy dogs won't want such a warm bed as some other breeds, terriers quite like a cozy den-like bed, many dogs like to curl up in a secure and safe feeling bed with sides. Also remember that puppies are quite likely to chew their beds so don't get the deluxe version straight away!! A bed that can be washed is useful and I always like my dogs to have a choice of bed and place to sleep depending on how they feel but that is personal preference. It is important that the bed is located in a quiet place where they can sleep comfortably and undisturbed.

🐾 **Rules & Boundaries**: think about what your rules are going to be. Is the puppy going to be allowed on the sofa? Where in the house do you want it to be able to go? It's easier for you and the puppy if you are consistent. As time goes on you can be more flexible if you want to be, but it's hard for the puppy to understand

if it's initially allowed in the whole house, on the sofa etc and all of a sudden it's confined the kitchen all the time. Make sure that everyone in the household knows what the rules are so that you can be consistent and prevent any anxiety or stress. You can't laugh and cuddle and reward a

playful puppy for exploring their way up and over chairs and onto a desk and then be cross with them when they do it on a different occasion and mess up your paperwork. Make rules that everyone is aware of, and your puppy will know where he stands (and that it probably shouldn't be on the desk!).

🐾 **Inappropriate mounting**: usually puppies and young dogs experiment with mounting behaviour when they are over-stimulated, too excited, stressed or over-tired, this can become a habit if the cause of the problem is not addressed. Sometimes in adolesence this type of activity can be hormonally based. Try to distract your dog away from what it's doing as other dogs are often not at all happy to be the recipient of this type of attention! If mounting is ignored or inadvertently rewarded it can develop into an embarrassing

habit and can put your dog at risk if it persists with a dog that isn't happy.

Don't hesitate to consult your vet, a professional dog trainer or behaviourist if you feel that the problem is getting worse or showing no sign of improvement.

🐾 **Hoovers, Mowers and Mixers**: very often puppies really don't like loud noises be it the vacuum cleaner, lawn mower or other noisy household item. It can be tempting to tease them but not a good idea in the long term as this can either lead to fear, over-excitement or aggression towards the appliance. Either have the puppy in a different room or introduce it to the appliance slowly. If the puppy approaches the hoover stop moving it and switch off, it can help for the puppy to be allowed to explore it in it's own time. In the communication chapter we looked at calming signals and you may notice your puppy using a lot of these (e.g. lip licking, yawning, displacement activities) when you use the vacuum cleaner so pay heed to these signals and stop what you're doing before the puppy feels the need to react. This can be the same with lawn mowers, sweeping, dusting and other household items and activities so give the puppy time to get used to anything that it's not sure about.

PUPPY EQUIPMENT

LEADS, HARNESSES, COLLARS ETC
SUITABLE & UNSUITABLE: THE WHYS & WHEREFORES

Whatever equipment you decide to use make sure that the dog or puppy gets used to it in the home first and is comfortable having it put on and taken off. Ensure you do this before you take it outside for the first time. The first time you put a collar or harness on, give the puppy something to do to take it's mind off wearing something new and initially only leave it on for a short period. You might put the collar or harness on and then give the puppy some scattered food or a kong for example. When starting to use a lead you might just walk around the kitchen or the garden a few times to get the puppy used to it in a gentle and calm way. Remember to make all first experiences as positive as possible.

The following equipment is categorised using simple traffic light colours, reflecting my thinking, opinions and experience based knowledge.

= YAY... Yes... You Betcha **!**

= Maybe... In some circumstances... Sometimes?

= No... Just no...No No **NO**. Step away from the item concerned.

Harnesses: personally I love harnesses for dogs and

puppies. A well fitting harness means that when the puppy is exploring the world it's not doing it with a lack of blood and oxygen to it's brain!! At first puppies are all over the place learning about their new surroundings and a harness means that they are not going to choke themselves or hurt their necks. The other advantage is that they are less likely to get the lead tangled under their legs and if you need to grab the puppy for any reason you can grab the harness not it's neck. When the puppy is growing you need to be aware that you may need to get a new harness every month or so but lots of them are adjustable so that they can last for a sensible amount of time.

Dogs also seem to be more comfortable having the lead attached to a harness rather than around their neck. There are a lot of different harnesses on the market so find one that is suitable for your dog's shape and size and one that you will find easy to use and put on.

🐾 **Leads**: long training leads mean that the puppy can explore happily, the ideal length is at least 5ft or 160 cms or longer. Trying to keep a dog or puppy close to you by having a short lead will make them want to lean away from you, it's a basic fact, try holding a friend or child close to you when walking and you will find they'll try to lean away as well! In the early days the puppy will want to explore the world and I think it's important that they be given the opportunity when appropriate and safe and of course, until you have a good recall (see page 95), use of the lead is imperative.

Left: long, loose lead, enjoying the view. GOOD!
Middle: walking calmly on a loose lead. GOOD! Right: very short lead. BAD!

🐾 **Collars (& ID Tags)**: when in a public place it's a legal requirement (Control of Dogs Order 1992) for dogs to wear a collar with an identity disc (ID tag) with your details on. Failure to do so can lead to prosecution and a fine of up to £5,000 (at the time of going to press). A flat collar that's not too narrow is more comfortable. Make sure that the collar isn't too tight and also that it doesn't go over the dog's head. Check it for comfort regularly as your puppy will grow quickly and you need to ensure that it never gets too tight.

A well fitting collar and
ID disc

🐾 **Head Collars**: these are based on the same principle as a horse's headcollar, the idea being that if you guide the head the body will follow. In reality these basically work by pulling the dog's head around when it tries to pull on the lead. Haltis are a popular example of the head collar. In some circumstances these can be useful but in my personal opinion using a headcollar is not a permanent solution. I believe it's best if this type of equipment is used in conjunction with training with the goal being that the dog learns to walk nicely on lead either on a harness or flat collar.

Dog Coupler: this is an item that connects two dogs together with one lead attached. This can make walking two dogs easier for the human but often the dogs can be forced to walk closer to each other than they would choose and it limits their freedom to explore. If you decide that this is something that suits you and your dogs, then perhaps consider using two  leads some of the time; thereby allowing them to choose how closely they walk to each other on some occasions. Take time to introduce dogs to this type of equipment and start with short periods of time coupled together. Watch for calming signals and signs that they are not comfortable.

Extender Leads: popular items that appeal to may owners because they provide the puppy or dog with a little more freedom. However the downside is that you don't have as much control as is ideal and other dogs and people can get tangled up in them. Another disadvantage is that there is constant pressure on the dog as the lead extends or retracts; this can make it then rather difficult to teach your dog to walk on a loose lead.

Clothing: people wear clothing and dogs wear their own coats! Dog's have no need to wear clothing unless you have a hairless dog or one with

 a very thin coat. If the dog needs to be kept warm there are suitable waterproof and fleece type garments for them which don't inhibit their movement or sight, and nor do they make a mockery of them. Some articles of dog clothing can make it difficult for them to communicate with other dogs and make other dogs misinterpret their signals so bear that in mind if you decide to get your dog a wardrobe.

Dog Perfume: words fail me! Dogs have an incredible sense of smell and masking their natural smell with dog perfume is unkind. Think about just how many humans get a headache around strong artificial smells such as air freshener or overly strong perfume and you may be able to begin to imagine how strong and unnatural smells may make a dog feel.

When we smell something too strong we can move away, but our dogs can't if they are wearing the problem! If your dog smells unpleasant you may need to look at it's state of health, stress levels and diet: a kinder and much healthier approach than perfume simply masking a pong.

Shock Collars: electric shock collars are another device that the Association of Pet Dog Trainers (APDT) and many enlightened trainers and owners are trying to get banned. The armed forces and the Association of Chief Police Officers (ACPO) have already imposed a voluntary ban on the use of these collars in their training. Independent scientific research confirms that their use is both painful and frightening, and that dogs can be damaged both physically and mentally by their use. I strongly advise people never to use these. If you have a severe problem with your dog seek professional advice. There are a lot of good and effective training methods you can use without giving dogs electric shocks.

Choke Chains: the APDT and many other professional organisations are trying to ban the sale and use of choke chains as they are unkind and can cause injury to the dog. Go to the APDT website (www.apdt.co.uk) for more information on how damaging their use can be and don't even think about buying one!

Spray Collars: there are a variety of spray collars on the market that claim to solve various problems including barking. But it's best to find out why the dog is barking in the first place and deal with the causes and not just the symptoms. When thinking of trying a device like this seek professional advice first and see if there is a better way from the dog's point of view to resolve the problem.

 **Muzzles:** some dogs are muzzled because they bite, but it's advisable to always seek professional advice to try and find out why they are biting and teach them to cope so that they don't need to resort to biting. Other dogs may be muzzled because they continually scavenge whilst out on walks. There are many different types of muzzle but for comfort and safety the type of muzzle where they can pant, drink and lip lick etc are preferable in many cases.

Go to the APDT website for up-to-date information on aversive training aids and consider all options before trying muzzles and similar equipment and think how the dog may feel if something harsh and confusing is used. Situations can actually be made much worse by using aversive methods.

WHAT TO LOOK FOR IN PUPPY CLASSES AND DOG TRAINERS

🐾 **Are they up to scratch and can they prove it?** When looking for dog or puppy classes, or for a dog trainer or behaviourist (or indeed for any other professional to work with you and your dog) check that they have appropriate and up-to-date knowledge. Also check that they are members of a professional organisation (e.g. Association of Pet Dog Trainers) and that they have relevant insurance. Most dog professionals continue to improve their skills annually through continued professional development (CPD) courses and reading to further their knowledge and handling techniques. Don't be bamboozled or fobbed off by spurious letters after their names, and unheard of organisational memberships. Look for recognised qualifications and memberships of known professional organisations.

🐾 **Are they up to date?** It makes sense to find someone whose skills and knowledge are as current as possible because methods, techniques and awareness change all the time. You wouldn't want to consult a vet or doctor whose skills, knowledge and equipment was out of date, old fashioned or rusty.   Equally you need to know that their knowledge, techniques and skills are based on learning, research, hands on experience and fact rather than tenuous hearsay.

🐾 **Do a recce:** if you are thinking of going to a class or puppy party ideally go along initially *without* your dog to see if you like what you see. At first this idea strikes some as odd, but you want your dog or puppy's first experience of class to be a good one, so this first recce or reconnaissance mission can reap great benefits.

🐾 **Size matters:** small classes are usually a lot less stressful and easier for you and your dog to cope with. The environment is very important as it needs to be calm in order for you and your dog to learn effectively.

🐾 **Be on your guard:** No reputable classes or trainers should advocate the use of choke chains, shock or spray collars, training discs, water pistols, tins filled with stones, hitting or shouting or any other aversive or shock tactics. If you feel that what you're being told to do isn't suitable for you or your dog don't be afraid to say so. Your priority is your dog's wellbeing.

In summary: Always do your homework to find the best people and places for you and your dog to learn. Many trainers and behaviourists provide details of how they work on their websites and/or will be happy to chat to you on the phone to explain in greater detail. We all learn best when we are relaxed and happy so finding the *right* trainer is vital.

STAGE 2: ADOLESCENCE
(6 - 24 months+)

Once a puppy has its adult teeth it is thought to have become an adolescent and at this stage they may become more challenging, have less concentration and be more confident. During adolescence all species (including dogs) get a lot of extra growth and sex hormones coursing through their system. Their breed instincts and drives will increase for example a Jack Russell puppy that has been happy to mooch about will start to be interested in squirrels, rabbits, cats etc and sniff a lot more and even shoot off chasing things.

A guarding breed of dog may start to bark at the door and defend it's territory or guard the family, bed or other pets in the home. The adolescent years in human development can be very difficult and go on for up to 10 years but the good thing about dogs (even larger ones) is that it lasts a lot less time than it does in humans.

Remember that dogs should not be running or jogging with you, doing agility or flyball type activities until they are fully grown and adult otherwise you can be doing them serious and long term physical harm.

🐾 Legs up, sniffing around, play fights and grrrrrrrrrrrrrowling
The sex-drive (one of the primary drives) will start to kick in and male dogs will start to raise their leg when they urinate rather than squat. They will also be a little more interested in all other dogs and smells left by other dogs. When testosterone is released into the system in greater amounts they may become more reactive and perhaps growl at other dogs or get growled at when they behave inappropriately. Older dogs are better than we are at telling dogs they're being irritating so don't worry if an otherwise polite and nice older dog growls at your adolescent, they are hopefully telling them politely but firmly not to be an idiot!

During adolesence it's advisable to watch out for play fighting escalating and going too far. Split up rough play as soon as possible and get the dogs to learn to walk sensibly together; sniffing and being functional and calm. As I've said before we don't encourage adolescent humans to continue to roll around on the floor play fighting and we shouldn't do so with dogs either. If they lived in family groups the older dogs would intervene but in the absence of older more sensible dogs in the group we (the owners) need to step in.

🐾 Understanding the appeal of urine & faeces

Bitches may urinate more on a walk as they start to mark to let other dogs know that they are around and potentially looking for a mate at some point. Urinating is an important aspect of communication for dogs and with their powerful sense of smell they can gain a lot of information about another dog including sex and state of health. The placement of urine and faeces becomes more important to them and they will get increasingly interested in all smells. Knowing what a powerful sense of smell dogs have, their desire to sniff around urine and faecal matter can seem counterintuative to humans, but on the other hand (or paw) dogs may think the same about some of the things we do!

🐾 Bitches' first seasons

Bitches are likely to come into their first season from about 8 months onwards and this will last for about 3 weeks during which time you should keep them away from male dogs. Even other bitches may behave differently towards them. I have observed that some bitches become either more reactive or a bit depressed around this time and generally it's not unusual for their moods to change and for them to be grumpy.

Neutering & Spaying

During a dog's adolescence owners usually think about spaying and neutering their dogs, and it's something to consider carefully and sensibly. It's advisable to speak to your vet and they will be able to guide you and advise you on the whole procedure, its impact and the best time to carry out

Please...
NEUTER YOUR PETS
AND
WEIRD FRIENDS & RELATIVES

the procedure if that's what you decide to do. More usually vets neuter after 6 months for dogs, however with bitches the timing can vary with some vets preferring to spay before the first season and some after the first season. (Remember bitches generally come into season anytime after 8 months and it can last for up to 3 weeks).

There are many health benefits to spaying and neutering along with the advantage of no unwanted litters of puppies. It is thought that a male dog can smell a bitch in season up to 5 miles away and as the sex drive is one of the strongest drives it may lead to intact males escaping from the house or garden and wandering or running off when you are out walking. The most important thing to avoid is unwanted and unplanned litters of puppies. To be honest it's best to leave breeding to those who have the appropriate knowledge; if you have any doubts about this just look at the at the dog shelters and rescue organisations over-flowing with unwanted dogs and puppies.

STAGE 3: ADULTHOOD

 Food... Diet... Weight...

Once a dog is adult and has stopped growing you need to make sure that the diet is appropriate for the dog's breed, level of exercise and state of health and that it doesn't gain excess weight. Dogs need more food when they are growing and as an adult it's important that have the appropriate adult food whether that is wet, dry, home-cooked or raw. It's a good idea to make sure that your dog has a general health check at the vet annually and perhaps pop in on a semi-regular basis for a free weighing session so that you can ensure that your dog doesn't carry excess weight, as this can impact quite seriously on their long-term health and mobility. Excess weight will also inhibit the dog's ability to attend to personal hygiene and clean itself which may lead to infection and ill health. Popping into the vet from time to time is a good idea anyway to make sure that the dog feels comfortable there.

The Big Boys Games

Once your dog is fully grown and adult (this varies with different breeds and sizes of dog) you can consider participating in 'new' activities together if you want to, these include: agility, jogging with your dog, field trials etc. In essence all of the more strenuous activities that aren't suitable for dogs until they are fully grown.

Time to grow up?

If your dog reaches adulthood and is still behaving like a puppy it's time to speak to a professional trainer or enrol in some classes. Any behaviour problems in an adult dog should be addressed quickly before they develop into something more serious. Prevention of problems in the first place is clearly the ideal but failing that, get to work on any issues before they become a habit that's harder to change.

Never too old to learn new tricks

Adult dogs are capable of continuing to learn throughout their lives. They can learn good things as well as bad things just like us, so don't ever think that once you've finished classes you no longer need to make any effort. We continue (hopefully) to learn throughout our lives and so do our dogs. Like any good relationship the ones we have with our dogs will take work to get the most out of them but it shouldn't be tedious or hard work.

Enjoy your adult dog, and help him continue to learn and grow with you.

Chapter Four

SOCIALISATION
How? When? Where?

Having a well socialised dog is extremely important as lack of good socialisation can lead to fear, behaviour issues, lack of confidence and sometimes aggression in adult dogs. Introducing your puppy, adolescent or adult dog to a variety of different situations in a calm and positive way will enable him to be able to cope in the many different circumstances he may encounter in the future.

The earlier that puppies start to be socialised the better, but it is never too late to start and it's something that you continue throughout their lives. If you stop and think about it, we never truly stop our socialisation process or learning; and it's the same for dogs. It's good to maintain and develop their social skills and keep improving them even as adults. Be aware though that moderation is needed and just like us, if they socialise too much or in the wrong type of way it can again lead to problems. It's all about balance and what's suitable and enjoyable for each individual dog.

Below are experiences and situations to consider when planning your puppy or dog's socialisation. Don't over-do it, and keep sessions short in the beginning. Plan what you are going to do, plan what you want to achieve and stop before the dog gets too tired, worried or over-stimulated.

🐾 People in General

It's important for dogs to meet people of all ages; human movement varies depending on age, state of health etc and you don't want (for example) a dog that barks at a wheelchair user, an elderly person with a walking stick or a small child. Remember dogs communicate a lot with body language and will be watching the body language of people that they meet. Dogs can become worried, over-stimulated or frightened if they perceive the body language in front of them them to be threatening, confusing, inflammatory or hostile. When socialising your dog think about introducing them to people in uniforms, carrying umbrellas, wearing hats or hoods etc. (Note: this doesn't mean that you need to go up to all of these people for 'formal introductions'!) Be aware of your dog's body language and if they appear worried distract them and increase the distance from whatever or whomever is worrying them. Slowly introduce your dog to larger groups of people and more crowded areas; though do this only for short periods of time in the beginning. Always keep an eye on your dog and watch out for any increase in negative signals or discomfort and if in doubt move away to a quieter area or go home.

🐾 Children

Getting your dog used to children is important as they can move in unpredictable ways and make some awful noises which can upset or frighten dogs and puppies. Also there seem to be an increasing number of children around who

are frightened of dogs. It's important to be able have control over your dog at all times, have a good recall and be able to encourage or distract them away. I don't encourage children to touch or feed my dogs as I don't want them to see children as a source of food or excitement. It's best if dogs socialise with the children they know and leave the others alone. Too often I see out of control dogs rushing up to children and snatching ice creams or sandwiches and it's just terrible to watch. It gets dogs and their owners a bad reputation and frightens children. Once a dog is taught that children are rewarding (in food or excitement terms) it means they are likely to go up to every child expecting something nice or a game and unfortunately that's not always the case.

🐾 Runners, Cyclists, Skateboarders, Horses & Riders, Scooters & more

Teaching your dog to ignore the other people using the parks makes for a happier time. The goal is a dog who is relaxed and confident as these streams of busy characters whizz by. This is a great example of where understanding your breed is so important: some breeds of dogs are hardwired to chase things that move. For example hounds, collies and terriers will be more predisposed to chasing a moving

target. Teach your dog from an early age to come away happily for a reward and to ignore the faster moving

characters they encounter (be they park, by-way, road or pavement users). This will lead to more harmonious walks. It can be very helpful to get friends to set up situations and to run or cycle past so that you can practice your distraction technique and recall away from different things.

🐾 Livestock

Early training not to chase any livestock is advisable. ('Livestock' being horses, cows, sheep, chicken, geese, ducks etc etc etc.) Dogs caught worrying sheep may be shot by the farmer or may face being euthanised by a vet. There are many commercial shoots around the country with lots of pheasants, partridges and ducks and the game keeper in these areas may well shoot a dog if it chases the game birds. A dog that chases horses or barks at them may not only be a

danger to itself but may cause a horse to bolt, run into fences, harm itself or throw its rider. So for the safety

Different species can get on very well

of all concerned training and socialising your dog with all types of livestock is essential. It's also not desirable for dogs to chase deer or birds, in some of the Royal parks this may result in a fine or worse.

🐾 Different Breeds & Sizes of Dogs

Where you live is likely to dictate just how easy this is to do. I remember the first time that my Parsons Terrier met a Pekingese in the park; his eyes were out on stalks and he approached with much trepidation and curiosity. Yet a couple of weeks later he passed the same Pekingese with an almost dismissive 'been there done that' reaction as he carried on his merry way. People are the same and if we see someone who looks different many of us will initally stare (a reaction that is most pronounced in children). Of course staring fixedly at something is as rude in human terms as it is in dog language, but sometimes we, and our dogs, can't help ourselves.

Remember some breeds that are particularly hairy (e.g. Pekingese, Old English Sheepdogs, Bearded Collies, Hungarian Pullis) or breeds which have shortened jaws (e.g.Boxers, British Bulldogs, Pugs etc) may make some of the more subtle body language signals harder to understand. This will add an extra layer of confusion for your dog as he comes to grips with the 'strange' dog in front of him. For example a head turn from a dog without much of a nose won't mean much or be a very obvious signal, equally with a very hairy dog some of the soft eye gestures or lip licking may be lost.

Bear in mind that where you have difficult communication you may not always have the most harmonious of encounters.

The other thing to be aware of, and get dogs used to, is the different body postures of some breeds. Boxers, for example, are bred with a very upright stance which can signal hostility to another breed.

As with all these experiences and situations, the more different breeds your dog meets, the more confident and able to cope your dog will be.

🐾 Traffic

If you live in the countryside and don't intend your dog to go anywhere far from home this may be less of an issue. However if you plan for your dog to travel with you or go on holiday to different places it's a good idea to get it used to different types of traffic. Thinking of the dog's powerful sense of smell and acute sense of hearing we can understand why heavy traffic may be unpleasant for them but they can get used to it.

Big lorries, buses, air brakes going off; all these things may be scary in the beginning. Start off gently and work up to exposing your dog to heavier traffic as they become more able to cope. Scooters and motorbikes can be a problem; in the beginning expose them to these types of vehicle and noise from a distance, then over time decrease that distance. Ultimately your dog will accept them as normal. Never force your dog; if he shows any signs of not coping increase distance and move away. (Signs may include tense body language, jerky movements, rapid yawning or lip licking.)

🐾 Travelling

Teaching your dog to cope with travel is a good idea as at some point you may need to transport your dog. With my own puppy I used to go and sit in the car with her and let her explore and feel comfortable being in it without even starting it up and going anywhere.

As I travel around a lot and like my dogs to be with me, it was important that she liked the car and felt comfortable with spending increasingly longer periods of time in it. We also practiced going on buses, only one stop in the beginning and building it up to several stops before getting off and walking home. The same with trains and picking the quiet times rather than rush hour so that the experience was a good one.

Now I find that my dogs take everything in their stride and are happy to travel in horse boxes, on trains, buses and cars but we haven't tried air travel yet. Because all of their experiences have been good when

travelling I have no doubt that if I did want to fly with them they would cope with it and I would spend time beforehand preparing them to spend time in a travel crate.

Loud Noises

Most dogs have better hearing than us, in fact some may have hearing that is so acute it's thought to be up to four times better than ours. The range of things that they can hear is much broader than ours as well. I know that sudden loud noises and especially loud music can hurt my ears and over time give me a headache; so consider your dog's comfort when exposing them to loud noises as it may hurt their ears and their heads too.

When introducing them to loud noises such as gun shots and traffic etc do it at a distance at first and decrease the distance slowly at intervals that suits the individual dog. Again any desensitization programme should be done slowly over a sensible period of time. Consider also your tone of voice and volume when speaking to your dog or training them, and be aware that shouting, screaming and cheering may well distress them. It's is worth thinking about how loud you have the television and music on in your home or your car. Remember if the dog can't get away from it, it may well make the dog feel uncomfortable; so be sure to be considerate.

Vets

It is possible for dogs to become frightened of the vet especially if the only time that they go there something painful or scary happens to them. Vets and the nurses very often go out of their way to make the experience a positive and happy one for the dog using food rewards and a slow and gentle approach. Many vets offer puppy parties as part of the socialisation experience. In fact I run puppy socialisation classes in my local veterinary surgery and find that puppies can't wait to get into the surgery. Without the opportunity of classes in the surgery many vets are happy for owners and their dogs to pop in to the surgery just to say hello, get weighed and have a treat; it helps to make going there positive.

The other thing that makes it easier for vets is to get your dog used to being examined by you, friends and other members of the household. Never force the dog but slowly get them comfortable with having their teeth and paws looked at and get them used to being touched all over. It's generally a good idea to check your dog over after a walk to check for burrs, thorns, grass seeds etc and to be able to inspect their ears, and eyes etc. So this is a good habit to get into generally.

🐾 Household Appliances

As discussed above, sudden loud noises can frighten dogs of any age. So bear this in mind when you switch something on. Watch for your dog's reaction and if it's upsetting them switch it off. My own dogs tend to walk in front of me when I'm hoovering as they try to calm the vacuum cleaner down. In their eyes the hoover is rude and noisy and needs to be calmed down and walking slowly in front of it is their way of trying to communicate peaceful and calm intentions with it. I deal with this by changing direction away from the dogs and taking breaks or even closing the door on the room that I'm doing so that they are not in the room at the

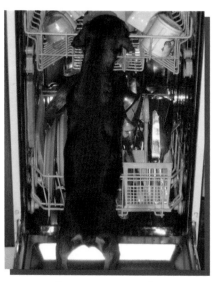

Puppy pre-wash

time. Try to not push the hoover towards the dog as this is confrontational and upsetting for them. Hairdryers can also be frightening for a dog so make sure that you never point the dryer at them and make sure they have an escape route if they need one to get away. Remember always stop what you're doing before the dog gets upset and if in doubt put the dog in a different room. Never force situations.

🐾 Street Markets, High Streets, Stations etc

Start early in the day before these areas get too busy and build up to taking them when it's busier. To enable your dog or puppy to be able to cope in many situations it's a good idea to build up their experiences in busier areas slowly and in short bursts. If you ever plan to take your dog to a dog show or any other busy event you want to ensure that they've had experience of crowds before.

Living in London I have access to crowds at any time should I choose it. But with a puppy I build the experiences up slowly and teach them to not jump towards strangers, and to be able to cope with increasing noise and numbers of people. Recently I took my 16 month old puppy to a small dog show with lots of people, noise and dogs. She was very calm and politely

Dog Show

interested in all the extraordinary things going on. Though she had never seen so many barking dogs who were struggling to cope with the situation and owners shouting and pulling etc! She was able to walk around feeling happy and confident and before it became too much we left.

 Always try to finish any new experience on a positive note and before your dog is tired or stressed.

The above suggestions include just a handful of experiences and situations to give you ideas. Overall you should make sure that all your puppy's (or dog's) experiences are positive and ensure that you reward appropriate good behaviour at all times. Avoid anything that might frighten the puppy or anything that might be unsafe. If your puppy or dog is frightened or having trouble coping take him away from the stressful situation. It is hard for anyone, including dogs and puppies, to learn and accept things when stressed so allow them time to figure some things out by themselves and experience different situations at least 3 to 5 times. Whatever you do don't force a puppy to do anything it's unsure of or afraid by.

Taking your dog out and about with you will introduce them to lots of new and interesting experiences

PUPPY SPECIFIC CONSIDERATIONS
What sort of dogs should my puppy meet?

Ideally you will introduce your puppy to well socialised and well behaved older dogs that are preferably over 2 years old.

Like many other species, including us, dogs learn in many ways but mimicking and example are easy ways to learn. When puppies are young they will learn bad habits and undesirable behaviours from other dogs if you allow them to. Certainly as child I sometimes found rebellious, cheeky and naughty friends fascinating and suffered the consequences when I copied that behaviour! One particular friend ended up being banned from our home and on reflection it was with very good reason. There are dogs that I see out walking that I don't want my dogs to meet and I certainly wouldn't invite them over for a social date. I prefer to think of my role in my dog's lives as a parenting one, guiding them to be well socialised, confident, able to cope and to make good decisions in all the many situations they will come across during their lives.

Continuous and unsupervised play with other puppies or adolescents may lead to over-excitement and over-tiredness, this is not always a constructive way to learn how to behave. Who is capable of making a good decision or behaving functionally when over-tired or over-stimulated? I know that I'm not. When your puppy meets older polite dogs it will learn how to communicate, interact and approach in a healthy and functional way. If the puppy bites an older dog too hard or behaves inappropriately the older dog will usually let the puppy know gently but firmly: older dogs are much better at teaching puppies than we are, afterall they 'speak dog'. (Although as we've discussed; with time, perseverance and a keen eye we can learn a great deal more about canine communication.) Older dogs give puppies a 'green card' for the first few months and are generally very tolerant of their behaviour and gentle so keep your lead slack and allow them to interact and learn. Note: adolescent dogs have their own issues (mostly to do with increased hormones) and may not be ideal companions for an impressionable puppy.

Very often in the park I see people letting their dogs off lead to run around and play with other dogs and they just feel happy that the dogs are having a good time and getting plenty of exercise with the thought that 'at least they will be tired when they get home'. As the play gets more rough and excited the dogs start to tire and movements can become jerky; some dogs may have had enough and be unable to extract themselves from the situation. It's important to understand the dangers of play continuing unchecked. We wouldn't allow children to just roll around play fighting until someone got hurt, tired or bullied and we shouldn't allow this with our dogs.

If they begin to associate the park with a wild and excited time they will pull on lead all the way to the park and then run off with no regard to you at all.

Behaviour rarely stays the same and certain behaviours will increase. Over time your dog may start to get even more excited at the prospect of a walk; they may jump around and behave madly before you even get out of the door. This can lead to recall problems and bullying behaviour in the park with younger or smaller dogs. If you drive to the park your dog may whine or bark on the way, in anticpation of the wild time to be had when they get there. Think of the wild time in the park as equivalent to taking a child to a fairground, is it easy to get a child to walk slowly into a fairground and listen to what you say? Are they relaxed and happy to put to be bed after an exciting time or in a position to learn anything? Consider this and draw your conclusions, then apply them!

A nice social walk with older dogs

PARK ETIQUETTE !

🐾 *"Oh don't worry ! Slasher's just being friendly !"*
Something that I struggle with when it comes to walking with my dogs (and more especially with client dogs who may have inter-dog problems) is the 'he's just being friendly' approach. There have been many situations where I ask someone to call their dog away from a client dog that is on-lead, a dog who is clearlystruggling to cope with a 'friendly' approach only to be told by the other owner "Oh my dog's fine!". The fact that their so called friendly dog has not picked up on the desperate 'keep away' signals from the struggling dog frustrates me greatly, and can only make a fearful dog more fearful.

If I went for a walk in the park with one of my nieces and a bigger and perhaps older child came up with overly friendly intentions and my niece didn't want to play or interact with them, but they persisted with trying to get my niece to do what they wanted it would be called bullying. No parent or child carer would put up with it so I wonder why do we think it's acceptable for dogs to have to put up with unwanted attention? I've lost count of the number of times I seen a young or frightened dog going behind the owner's legs to avoid unwanted attention from another 'friendly' dog only be to pulled forward to meet the antagonist. In these situations the owner should think about how their dog feels, watch their signals and use themselves as a barrier, effectively physically splitting their dog from the unwanted attention and definitely not forcing an unwilling meeting.

Overly enthusiastic and overly familiar greetings between dogs (and people!) are uncomfortable and are to be avoided. "He's only being friendly" is not an excuse that means you can allow your dog to force itself on others. Take responsibility for your dog's actions. As you learn more about canine communication you will see how much distress is caused by unwanted attention and some dogs not listening to others. Not being listened to or understood is extremely upsetting whatever species you are.

🐾 Protect your dogs: In the case of some un-neutered males approaching other dogs head on, it is sometimes most definitely not friendly, and certainly not innocent, and is in fact more likely to be sexual harassment which can be frightening and overwhelming for many dogs. In these instances we must put the dogs in our care and their feelings first, and not be afraid to ask other owners to call their dogs away even if they do tut and think we are being rather over protective of our dogs. I know that if I were to get approached by an overly amorous male who was checking me out and pestering me in an open and clearly sexually aggressive manner I would dearly hope someone would be around to help me! How awful if people just walked past and told us to deal with it like it was our problem not the sex pests'! We teach our children and adolescents how to behave politely and appropriately and what's acceptable and what's not: this should be translated to our dealings with dogs so that they don't learn to intimidate, bully and frighten others. Even when your dog reaches adulthood, you will need to monitor your dog's behaviour in case bad habits creep in. We continually adjust our own behaviour all of our lives so that we can live happily and harmoniously and cope with all situations. We need to encourage and facilitate the same in our dogs.

I watch my own dogs constantly when out walking: that way I can see if I need to pick up poo, I can monitor their meetings and greetings and see if I need to help them out by splitting or call them away from any potentially difficult situations. This is called common courtesy and being polite. My own dogs are very capable of dealing with most situations as am I, but it's nice to feel that we have back up and support when we need it.

And it should go without saying but do be a responsible dog owner: carry poop bags and use them. (This is a sign from Frankfurt: very detailed signage the Germans go for)

Recently I observed a young Labrador with a jogger, as the owner jogged past wearing headphones, the puppy (who shouldn't have been jogging at such a young age) stopped to engage with my dogs and by the time the puppy and I looked up, the owner was nowhere in sight. I walked along hoping to catch sight of the owner so that I could indicate to her that her dog was with me. It was nearly 5 minutes later before the owner came back into view, but her puppy had run off in a panic to try and find her. I pointed out where the puppy had gone and stated that the dog had lost her. The owner was cross and told me that the dog was perfectly capable of finding her and turned and ran off. Moments later there was hooting of cars and I saw that the puppy was running in the nearby main road looking for her owner and the owner had failed to hear what was going on as she still had her headphones on. After some frantic shouting and gesticulating the owner looked over to the road and ran over to retrieve her dog from a kind spirited and helpful passer-by. This is sadly not an unusual situation in London and probably in many other areas of the country. When you are with your dog I suggest not having long mobile telephone conversations or listening to music; we wouldn't do that if we walked with a friend or a child and it's unsafe and irresponsible to do so with a dog. Keep your dog in sight at all times so that you can react and help them out if you need to.

When people jog with their dogs or walk along on the phone or with headphones on they are mostly unaware of what's going on and fail to pick up poo, notice if their dog is in danger or having a problem, scavenging from the bins or being a menace to others.

🐾 **Food theft**: I love dogs and spend the majority of my time either with them, thinking about them, talking about them, working with them or writing about them but I do object to dogs running up to me and jumping at me and trying to mug me for food.

Humans don't generally grab food from each other (except in fun or criminal acts!) and well adjusted, polite dogs don't grab food from each

other either.   I have had owners who basically shrug off their
dog's rude behaviour by saying 'you must have food on you' as if
it's my fault that their dog jumped on me! I expect to be able walk
unmolested in the park and on the streets, carry food rewards for my
dogs and maybe even food for me and not have someone else's dog harass
or jump on me. Children also have a right to use the park and to be able to
feed the ducks without having the bag of bread snatched from them or at
worse to be knocked over by a strange dog.   Pushchairs and buggies often
have food items in them and we wouldn't go up and help ourselves to other
people's food and neither should our dogs. Similarly
we wouldn't go and help ourselves to a selection of
goodies from someone else's picnic, it is just as
unacceptable for your dog to think he can do
so. Basic training or keeping your dog on
lead can prevent these types of problem
occurring and training with the right trainer
can be fun for all involved.

Take responsibility for your dog's behaviour and if it's not behaving
appropriately, accept that it's your problem as the owner, and is not other
people's. For some reason, use of the lead seems to be a last resort for many
dog owners. In fact it should be the first port of call, a dog that learns to run
around and behave badly will only get better at it the more it's allowed to
practice doing so.

In short when socialising and out and about teach your dog good manners.
It's not hard but it's hugely rewarding when you can take your dog anywhere
and everyone finds your dog a joy to be around.

Chapter Five

STRESS

> *You have no idea the day I've had! First the cat knocked over my water bowl, then my bone got stuck under the sofa, then the postman kept ringing and ringing the door bell, then the rope on my 'ball on a rope' snapped and as if that wasn't bad enough the squeaky beak came off my rubber chicken.*
> *Grrrrrr grrrr grrr*

> *Have you tried chasing your own tail and getting your tummy tickled? Always works for me...*

Salivating and stressed from too much fun

When I first learned about stress in dogs I felt terrible when I realised I'd made some huge mistakes with my current and past dogs. On courses about 'stress in dogs' I've witnessed owners actually cry during the course, and countless others express how bad they felt; how guilty. You must remember that learning about a topic such as this is positive and constructive. Don't feel bad, instead focus on positive emotions. Be pleased you're learning more about your dog, and you're going to be able to look at your situation and start to make some positive (but gradual) changes for you and your dog.

In my own case I've found and continue to find learning about stress hugely empowering and interesting as it has such a huge impact on us, both emotionally and physically. Looking back at various periods in my life I was clearly extremely stressed, suffered ill health, and did all sorts of things that were fairly destructive in one way or another, but at the time I didn't think I was that unhappy, I just didn't know any better. Now I can look back and think *"Thank goodness"* I made positive changes to my life and my dogs' lives.

Change needs to be made gradually, with the goal clearly being no stress at all; but be realistic and accept that none of us can live in Utopia. Personally speaking I still get stressed sometimes, but the big difference is that I recognise it now and know what to do. My dogs don't live stress free lives but we try to maintain a sensible balance and have fun. Please read about stress with an open mind and don't allow the voices in your head to berate you for past things you can't change. If you want to explore stress and its impact on us and our dogs there are many good books on stress on the market, some of which are recommended on pages 104 & 105.

STRESS: THE BASICS

Let's start off discussing human stress as stress affects all animals, including humans, in a similar physiological way. In laymans' terms stress can also be 'catching' so if we are stressed there is every chance that our dog (and family) might be stressed as well. Certainly I don't feel very comfortable spending time around someone who is extremely stressed: generally I want to get as far away from them as possible but if I can't, their behaviour may make me feel irritated, worried, frightened and generally stressed!

Like it or not statistically the country is losing approximately 360 million working days annually due to ill health and at least half of that ill health is attributed to stress which is estimated to be costing UK industry approximately £4 billion and rising! Is stress on the increase? Is stress all in the mind? Many people really don't really like the word or the fact that so many things are now attributed to it. But the fact is that stress has always been around it's just we are now more aware of it, and therefore label it more accurately.

Excessive stress affects our ability to do our jobs, can cause us to make mistakes and have accidents and also affects our relationships and emotional health not to mention our physical health. Indeed when stress continues for any period of time it can seriously impact upon our physical, emotional and and psychological well being in wide variety of ways.

🐾 What is stress?

🐾 Broadly speaking researchers in the field define stress as:
'a physical, mental, or emotional response to events that causes bodily or mental tension.'

Stress is unique to each of us: some of you might feel stressed at the thought of having to give a talk to a group of people or write a book! To some people it's stressful to cook for a large number of guests, whilst for others it's an enjoyable experience. Stress is uniquely individual and it's all about balance. In very simple terms stress occurs when we cannot cope and/ or things are out of balance. In just a few generations our lifestyles have completely changed and the demands placed on all of us have increased. To pick just a few examples of significant changes: we tend not to have jobs for life anymore, our diets are radically different, we have more pollution, our expectations are that we not only *could* but *should* have it all in terms of families and careers. We're all constantly juggling a vast array of demands on our time which causes great stress, and yet, paradoxically, it's been shown that boredom can be as stressful as a frenetic life.

Stress is commonly used in a metaphorical rather than literal or biological sense. To describe oneself or a colleague or friend as 'stressed out' is fairly commonplace vernacular. We tend to use it negatively, but as researchers over the years have agreed; in certain circumstances stress may be experienced positively. For example when our bodies and our brains respond to emergencies, and when a fight or flight response kicks in, a variety of chemicals are released into our systems. This then enables us to deal with, or escape from, something dangerous or frightening thus ensuring survival. In such circumstances stress actually enhances physical and mental performance over a short period of time, and can give us the strength to get away from a potentially dangerous situation or to stand and fight.

🐾 So, stress isn't always a bad thing !

Stress is essential for us and for animals to function: stress in the right levels at the right time is actually constructive. With the right levels of stress we are able to perform effectively and well in situations, it can be the thing that drives us every day, keeps us stimulated, makes us successful and can actually prolong our lives. The problems and negative impacts of stress only arise when we are under too much stress.

> *"No pressure, no diamonds."*
> *Thomas Carlyle*

🐾 Hmmm. So, how much is too much?

A great difficulty in defining 'too much stress' is due to the fact it is so subjective; one man's source of motivation is another man's worst nightmare. Personally I need deadlines to make me work more efficiently, but give me *too many* deadlines and pressures and I become stressed. For me the symptoms are that I become irritable, angry, clumsy, forgetful, restless and suffer from insomnia. Clearly when the balance goes awry we are not as effective as we could be and we make mistakes. Common symptoms are feelings of fear, fright and nausea, a propensity to sweat and cry, becoming forgetful, becoming aggressive, some people recede into their shells. Clearly you need to recognise your own symptoms as there can be no single broad brush diagnosis.

A Classic Stress Generator: The Pressure to Perform

Performance pressure can be divided into 3 groups and can be applied to dogs as well as humans.

3 Types of Performance Pressure:

Low pressure: under stimulated and bored. This is where we may be tired, and suffer feelings low energy and listlessness. If this state continues we become frustrated, dissatisfied, over sensitive, paranoid, bored and can't be bothered. We may also suffer low morale, illness, lack of productivity and produce poor quality work: this state is stressful in a bad way(!).

Optimum pressure: effective performance. The clue is of course in the name: in this state we should feel energised, creative, healthy, positive and enthusiastic. We should be less prone to sickness or infection, able to make decisions, have a desire for success, be able to produce a good standard and quality of work, be productive, be able to cope with change, feel satisfied, sleep well and enjoy our lives in a confident and functional way. This is where we and our dogs need to spend most of our time.

High pressure: over stimulated and pressurised. When in this zone you may feel uptight, irritated, have low self-esteem, exhausted all the time and be prone to make bad decisions. Quality of work and/or productivity will suffer, we suffer increased illness, are likely to struggle with the smallest of things, we can't handle changes at home, in relationships or at work and may be sensitive to sound, touch and generally tense. This is the state most people associate with 'being stressed'.

Positive Stress vs Negative Stress

Positive stress is there when we're coping, succeeding and feeling good. Negative stress is there when we can't cope, feel bad and things go wrong. Positive stress is important: it's normal, natural and keeps us within our coping abilities. Stress is only a problem if the body gets stuck in a bad place or position and uses resources in an unbalanced way. There are two systems, our sympathetic which manages our flight or fight mechanism and our parasympathetic which deals with 'housekeeping'; healing, repair and growth. When a constant state of stress occurs the general housekeeping of the body gets slack and disease creeps in. The body is designed to go in and out of stress but needs respite periods to rest and heal.

It's all about balance. For example dogs that pull on lead may be stressed and out of balance. If you distort the body the organs can't work properly and health deteriorates. It's the same with people; if we sit slumped in a chair at a desk for long periods of time our digestion and general health may be impaired.

Being startled can cause stress, and is a good example of a reason for raised adrenaline levels. Of course a bit of adrenaline sometimes is great; we need it in many circumstances to enable us get up and generally function. Adrenaline and the associated hormones are essential to give us that extra help to perform well at a particular task and it's the same for our dogs. Too much and performance, thinking and coping may be impaired. But we'll look at adrenaline in more detail later in this chapter (see page 71).

🐾 What can be changed and what can't?

Environmental and chemical pollutants take their toll on us and dogs. When stressed and overloaded our sympathetic nervous system is in control and the body's housekeeping will be fairly non-existent, so it will store any toxins until the parasympathetic system takes over and can deal with them. Overload, illness and disease can result from a build up of toxins in our bodies. Chemical stress can occur in us and in dogs; stop and think about your dog: is he in the best health? If he suffers less than optimal health you need to play detective to find out the cause. A simple and straightforward example is to consider household chemicals. Some of these have been linked to asthma and eczema in people so think what they could be doing to your dog. Grooming chemicals (including shampoos etc) for dogs can again cause problems, think about strong smells and how they can make us feel (and remember a dog has a better sense of smell than us!) Car and home plug-in air-fresheners certainly give me a headache very quickly and are made from synthetic and sometimes toxic ingredients. Imagine the impact these smells may be having on our dogs. Think before you use any scented products around your dog.

Of course stress can be caused by many outside influences including frightening, emotional or exciting events and pain. For example, going to a party can be both exciting and scary or even emotional, depending on whom you might meet there. Furthermore the physical and emotional energy utilised means that whilst an occasional party or late night is fine, a whole week of good times will likely result in some signs of stress. Going to a fairground for a child can be very stimulating and exciting (of course some of the rides may be a little scary), but overall they will really enjoy themselves. Yet spending too long there will often result in tears, and going too often may (although most children would have you believe otherwise) result in signs of stress.

🐾 Making Sense of Senses

We take in all manner of sensory information through our eyes, nose, ears, mouth and touch. All this information is taken to the brain where it's processed (this is in both human and canine brains). Sometimes too much information goes into the brain, but the important things stick and the unimportant 'stuff' is filtered out. To be honest so much information goes into the brain all the time that it's essential that some of the unimportant stuff is filtered out. Though we hopefully remember the important things! Of course 'important' isn't just stuff like bank details and pin codes; it's also our brain remembering that boiling water scalds, and toxic fumes from cleaning mateials can burn your throat. We'll also remember if a certain road is one we would not go down late at night for reasons of personal safety; very similarly if a rabbit hops down a path and runs into a fox or a dog and has to run for its life, its brain will definitely remember where that path was so that it doesn't go there again! The rabbits brain will also ensure it remembers any good strategies used to out-run the fox or dog. The rabbit's brain will most likely filter out any irrelevant information gained on that journey and just remember the main event and no doubt the desire for future avoidance of foxes and dogs will have been reinforced.

🐾 Hunter or Prey?

Its argued by many that we are all preconditioned to be hunter or prey, to fight or take flight. But of course; which of those two we will be, and whether to fight or take flight depends not only on who we are, but who or what we are facing and all the circumstances that surround the encounter. Think about small children, they may be super confident and in charge (maybe even bossy) when with their baby brother at home; but that same child may well behave entirely differently at school towards the 'big boys and girls'. Even animals that are classically regarded as prey often decide to put up a fight when there is no escape route and thus flight is not an option. You have to look at the whole picture and all the influences.

Causes of Stress

In essence inability to cope with certain stimuli combined with being exposed to those stimuli too often, is the primary cause of stress. Of course the ability to cope in the first place is very individual, both for us and our dogs. Good examples of causes for both humans and dogs include high or unreasonable demands, too much or too little exercise and nagging.

Of course whilst many things contribute to our dogs becoming stressed, too much excitement or over-stimulation are classic sources of stress that owners frequently overlook. For example telling our dogs that we're going for a walk, but doing so in an excited way, is not always such a good idea.

Certainly not if it means that they are in a state of high excitement as they rush out of the door and into the street. Dogs that start the walk in an excited and over-stimulated way are more likely to pull on lead, bite at the lead, lunge at other dogs or jump up at strangers. Waving the leash around, speaking to them in the car in a highly animated fashion, and exciting them alerting them to the fact that you're going to the park or off to see such-and-such a friend may make them start to pant, whine or bark in the car.

Speaking to them in an excited and stimulating way, "Look! Who's that?!" whilst gesticulating wildly, or "Ooooh look there's a cat! See the cat! Can you see the cat?!" encourages over-excitement so that the moment you get out of the car, or out of the front door or the moment you let them off the lead they run around madly and perhaps behave inappropriately towards other dogs or people. Squeaky toys, excessive ball play, throwing sticks can all work your dog up into a hyper state, and the end result may well be stress. By doing these things we are building up their expectations, winding them up and making them reactive and putting them out of balance. Again some excitement is good but it's about balance and stopping before they get over-excited, over-stimulated or over-exercised. When children get over-excited we tend to distract them and calm them down by doing something else: we need to remember that when dealing with our dogs.

🐾 What stresses *YOU*?

Classic sources of stress for us include: lack of time, driving in rush hour, road works, family issues, being late, crowds, noise, tiredness, doing too much, unreasonable demands at work or home, being told what to do all the time, deadlines, computers crashing, arguments, bad diet, pain, flying, travelling, traffic jams, money, bills, relationships, lack of choice, too much responsibility, not being understood or listened to, frustration, exhaustion, fear... let's face it this list could go on ad infinitum. However as I've said before (and will say again) stress and the causes of stress are very individual.

🐾 What stresses your *DOG*?

Again this list could frankly fill a whole book on its own, and you may also find that the very things that stress our dogs are things that you feel are causes of stress for you too. You'll have thought of many of them I'm sure, but you may be surprised at those you've missed (the list is of course far from exhaustive).

✤ Pain or illness
✤ Not enough rest
✤ Too hot or too cold
✤ Too much of anything e.g. exercise, training, ball games, stimulation, attention, play
✤ Too little of anything e.g. stimulation, exercise, food, water, attention

A look of stress

✤ Inconsistency, be it in training, rules, food, routine etc
✤ Teasing: a bit of a game is fine sometimes but in needs to be appropriate and fair
✤ Not enough space to move around
✤ No choices: no say in length of walk, where to sleep, how long to sleep, when to eat etc
✤ Boredom
✤ Being too restricted: perhaps crated or kenneled for long periods of time
✤ Fear of consequences, punishment, loud noises, people, other dogs etc
✤ Over-crowding: too many dogs or people in the home
✤ Arguments or friction in the home: this can be between the humans or between dogs that don't get on
✤ Over-controlling owner: perhaps being told what to do all the time and too many demands
✤ Not being understood and lack of communication
✤ Lack of toileting opportunities
✤ Environmental factors which can include noise, pollution, cleaning products, air fresheners
✤ Going to the vet or the groomer or pet dog training classes, agility, flyball, the postman!
✤ Choking and pulling on lead, the wrong equipment i.e. choke chains, shock collars
✤ Aversive training methods, shouting, hitting, pushing, pulling, jerking
✤ Prescribed medications often have side effects

❁ Too much food or too little or even the wrong type of food for the breed, age and state of health

❁ Incorrect socialisation: be that not enough, the wrong type, or too much

❁ Travelling by car, van, bus or train

❁ Hectic rushed lifestyle

❁ Kennels (see later in this chapter, page 78, on choices for your dog when you go away)

❁ Sexual urges: it's thought that an intact dog can smell a bitch in season nearly 5 miles away. The sex drive is the strongest urge and may cause symptoms of extreme stress

General Signs & Symptoms of Stress

As we've discussed, stress can manifest itself physically, emotionally and/or mentally.

Physical The physical manifestions of stress occur when the body as a whole starts to suffer as a result of a stressful situation. Symptoms can be very varied, in both type and severity. The most common physical symptom in humans is headaches. This is thought to be because stress causes us to unconsciously tense our necks, foreheads and shoulder muscles. But in the long term stress can lead to all manner of problems including heart disease, high blood pressure, insomnia, fatigue, hair loss and digestive problems to name but a few.

Emotional When stress affects our minds the symptoms include lack of concentration, frustration, irritability, anxiety, and escalate up to anger, depression and memory loss.

Psychological Long-term stress can lead to psychological problems in some individuals. Manifestations include phobias, compulsive behaviours, eating disorders and withdrawal from society.

Dog Specific Signs & Symptoms

❁ Panting and/or sweaty paws

❁ Biting at the lead and other problem behaviours

❁ Pulling on lead or lunging at other dogs or people

❁ Inability to concentrate or learn

❁ Clumsy movements

❁ Shallow breathing

❁ Shutting down or hyperactive

❁ Urinating a lot or not at all, diarrhoea and digestive upsets

* Barking or whining or perhaps completely silent and withdrawn
* Destructive tendencies
* Obsessive behaviours which could include licking, barking, self mutilation, pacing, spinning round, tail chasing, shadow chasing
* Excessive salivating: dependent on breed, some breeds just salivate a lot so you need to know your dog and what's normal for the breed and specifically for him
* Inappropriate sexual and mounting behaviour
* Red eyes, dull eyes, rapid eye movement, very dilated pupils
* Ears may be hot, dirty or inflamed
* Smell: dogs smell unpleasant when they are stressed (diet may play a part in smell as well)
* Head may be hot
* Stiffness in the joints and when moving: general tension in the body
* Dandruff or excessive coat shedding, scratching
* Drinking a lot or not at all
* Noise or sound sensitive, hiding from noises or alerting to the slightest noise
* Touch sensitive
* Deafness: doesn't hear anything as shut down or too distracted
* Aggression and overly reactive
* Illness, allergies and ...(worst case scenario) even early death

Stress & Hormones

How does an adrenaline burst work and what hormones are released during this time? When an event happens adrenaline is released along with electrical impulses and many different hormones which gives us the strength and speed to deal with fighting or fleeing or freezing (some people or animals will in fact go extremely still and not be able to move this can be good or bad depending on the situation!). Basically it's thought that a single event can release a flood of these hormones and impulses into the system. It takes only minutes but recovery from this one event back to a normal level can take up to 6 days. It's easy to see how we can move quickly into a state of long-term stress and why for a few days after an event we might be more reactive. Below I describe just a few of the hormones that are released.

Adrenaline: makes the muscles active, and is essential to get away from a dangerous situation. In caged animals we may see constant pacing and repetitive behaviours; often that type of behaviour is a result of long term stress. Luckily we don't often see pacing animals in our zoos anymore as mental stimulation and games are used to keep them active and not bored or stressed. Following an event you can't turn off the adrenaline and it will carry on being released for many minutes depending on the stressor. Digestion slows when blood flow is directed elsewhere and acidity increases which if in long term stress can cause ulcers and digestive disorders as a result of increase in acidity.

Sex hormones: when testosterone is released it can lead to anger, rage, irritability, increased aggression and inappropriate mounting or increased sexual behaviour.

ADH (anti-diuretic hormone): stress causes the release of ADH which controls water balance, when our water balance becomes disrupted it may cause our bodies to get rid of water which leads to more urination and sweating – this is normal. Have you ever experienced a dog or puppy urinating when you get home or when visitors arrive? Dogs don't sweat through their skin like us so excessive urination, panting, sweaty paws or diarrhoea are common results of ADH release.   Have you ever noticed yourself getting sweaty hands or arm pits, running to the bathroom or drinking a lot when stressed, excited or anxious? Whenever I do talks I get very nervous and fidget, need to drink a lot of water or tea, run to the loo regularly and my hands are clammy. At least now I know why I do all these things and am very conscious of them and can take steps to reduce my anxiety.

Cortisol: a hormone released in adrenaline and long term release of cortisol can produce skin problems and allergies. Cortisol is released in excessive amounts when the body is under stress and can cause muscle tissue to break down and blood sugar to rise as well as damaging brain cells hence affects learning and memory.

When you have stressful event after stressful event the balance goes and you end up with long term stress which is the one thing we don't want.

When extremely frightened dogs may run away and hide, they can be gone for several days and they stay hidden and shut down until the adrenaline levels come down. During this time the dog has virtually shut down and is in shock so won't hear you calling its name; this is natural and their body's way of coping. When humans feel very frightened or anxious we like to feel safe and may hide in our beds or homes until we feel better able to cope.

Bad stress =
irritability, anger, inappropriate responses, stomach upsets,
very reactive, defensive, touch sensitive, sleeplessness.

Look at dogs in competition; as they leave the ring they sometimes try to lunge at other dogs on their way out as they are extremely reactive due to the stress impulses and hormones running through their systems. Years ago I used to ride competitively and my performance anxiety would make me get upset at the slightest thing and I would be highly irrational (though luckily I had a very understanding mother who would do her best to keep me calm before and after the competition). After a competition or similar event we often take time to rest ourselves and our animals to enable recovery to take place, in daily life we don't always think about that. There are many situations where we should just take that recovery time; 'time out' if you will.

Stress is not dangerous when it occurs just now and then, and we certainly can't control it or punish it so we must know about it and respect it. We should allow our dogs time to calm down after a stressful or exciting episode so that they don't need to defend themselves or be overly reactive.

After a major stressor, peace and quiet is essential. Remember that training may be quite a stressor so perhaps don't do any training after a stressful event as the dog won't be in a position to learn or even listen. Think about ball play, agility or class and how excited or stressed your dog gets during these sessions. Perhaps consider only doing this type of activity once a week or once a fortnight; whatever suits your individual dog. Give your dog up to a week to allow stress levels to come down after a very stressful event. Gentle slow walks, nosework, mental stimulation or gentle social walks will help: no rushing around!

This time out time is easily identiable in natural behaviours: wild dogs and wolves need an adrenaline rush to help them make their kill but they chew and relax for a long time afterwards and don't run around apart from when hunting (unless they're young). Chewing is particularly important after a meal as it makes the dog feel relaxed and releases feelgood endorphins: raw bones, dried fish, rawhide chews or filled Kongs are all good for dogs to encourage licking and chewing to make them feel good and aid the body's return to normal balance.

Long term stress levels occur when humans or dogs don't have time to calm down and relax and recover. In this situation their immune systems become compromised and they become prone to illness, infections and general sickness. Stress also causes hyperactivity and many problem behaviours and a general inability to cope or even think.

Preparing yourself or your dog for an exciting or stressful event will take thought and preparation, but it will enable you to perform well and to cope better. Clearly if you or your dog are in a state of long-term stress it will compromise performance. Short term adrenaline that's produced will help performance for the specific event. A greyhound for example that suffers from long term stress will be unable to cope with the excitement at the track and may go to pieces before the race whereas a dog that is fairly calm until just before the start may have a better race and will certainly recover more quickly and be healthier as a result. Recently at a dog show I watched an agility competition and the owners that got their dogs really hyped up, pulled them about and raised their voices (clearly stressed and suffering from performance anxiety(!)) tended to get the dogs into a confused and anxious state. These dogs then made mistakes in the ring. In life and any competition it's teamwork and good communication that are the keys to success.

Teaching our dogs to cope in a variety of different situations can help to prevent stress. We need to build up their ability to cope with lots of good and positive experiences. Occasional stress is fine, and indeed normal, after all we need to live and get on with our lives, but long term stress isn't acceptable or desirable for anyone.

STRESS REDUCTION STRATEGIES
(And How to Make Your Dog Feel Grrrreat!)

Once we know what stress is, what causes it, and what it looks like we can then start to look at how to keep the balance and reduce stress and aid recovery from stressful, fearful, over-stimulating, tiring or exciting events. By identifying what stresses your particular dog (and you) you are in a position to be able to take action. Of course this action will differ for all breeds and individual dogs.

Being understood is a big deal and is vitally important. As we've established, learning how dogs communicate is essential for anyone who has anything to do with dogs be they professionals (vets and veterinary nurses, behaviourists, trainers, breeders, those who work in dog rescue, judges, complementary therapists) and be they pet owners.

The following list suggests things that may help to reduce stress and perhaps make our dogs feel good.

How to Make Your Dog Feel Grrrreat!

🐾 Give your dog lots of praise and love (make it appropriate and consistent)

🐾 Make your dog feel safe

🐾 Ensure your dog has some peace and quiet: plenty of opportunity for undisturbed rest

🐾 Provide companionship: dogs are social creatures and don't enjoy long periods of isolation

🐾 Provide adequate, regular and suitable exercise for the dog taking into account breed, age, state of health, general fitness, energy levels etc

🐾 Avoid stressful encounters too often and give time between events for stress levels to reduce

🐾 Set your dog up for success

🐾 Provide escape routes where possible when a stressful situation arises

🐾 Give your dog the opportunity to toilet at will

🐾 Don't tell your dog what to do all the time

🐾 Provide a regular routine: regular meals, regular walks help to reduce anxiety in some dogs

Puppies sharing a bone

🐾 Make sure you'e offering good owner management: help your dog out, constantly strive to improve the relationship

A great chewing session does wonders for stress as this Manchester Terrier knows

🐾 Protect your dog from children(!) and teach children boundaries around dogs; children are great learners

🐾 Make sure you know how to use barriers and learn or develop good handling techniques for all situations

🐾 Ensure your dog enjoys good health and freedom from pain and illness

🐾 Great grub! Make sure your dog's nutritional needs are met, and that all his nutrition is suitable, balanced, appropriate and is enjoyed!

🐾 Got a problem? If your dog seems to be stressed, but you don't know why keep a diary making a note of everything that happens during the day (however small these things might be). A 24 hour diary can be enough to get a good idea of what's going on but keeping it weekly is better. You'll soon be able to narrow down and deal with the sources of the stress.

🐾 Take away unnecessary responsibility from the dog. For example if your door bell is a trigger that is causing your dog great distress, take charge of the situation and switch off the door bell or change it for one that doesn't distress your dog.

🐾 In multi-dog households look at how much play they have, how excited they get, and keep an eye to identify if there's any friction in the group that needs to be addressed.

🐾 Give your dog gentle massage: long slow stroking on a daily basis (so long as your dog enjoys it) for 15 to 20 minutes can be hugely pleasurable for your dog. Stroking and touch helps to release feel good endorphins in the dog and improves your owner-dog relationship. Do remember to watch for any signs that the dog is not comfortable with what you're doing. Quite often we unthinkingly touch quite roughly and in a stimulating way; keep touching light and gentle.

🐾 Make good use of filled Kongs and bones: give your dog access to things to chew and lick. This releases positive endorphins that make them feel good.

🐾 Look into flower essences if this appeals; they can help with many conditions but do take advice from someone who is appropriately qualified to advise on their use with dogs.

🐾 Explore essential oils; but only under supervision of someone who is qualified in prescribing essential oils specifically for dogs.

🐾 Crucially reduce owner or family stress: of course this is for your own sake too! But remember your dogs pick up on the stress around them.

🐾 Make time to sit quietly with your dog; it's good for both of you.

🐾 Find outlets for their instinctive behaviour e.g nosework, hide & seek, tracking, swimming (all this is of course dependent on age, health, breed etc).

Sometimes the most goosebump inducing clichés actually contain great advice, and clichéd as it may sound: "Time out", "Chill out time" or time to "kick back" is the best stress buster, as these dogs know all too well....

Taking time to enjoy the view

Chewing helps to reduce stress

Puppies, especially, need a bed in a quiet safe place and access to things to chew

Quality rest is important

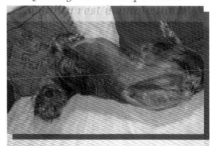

Room for two in a bed...

Relaxed border terrier

Now... that's relaxed...

Glorious mud! Wallowing happily

HOLIDAYS & STRESS

Urban mythology has it that somewhere, at some time, research has shown that the five biggest sources of stress (in no particular order) are: weddings, death, divorce, Christmas and holidays. Now whilst our stress is based on getting to the airport on time, or packing everything we need, or making sure the newspapers are cancelled, or maybe even the problem of paying for the whole thing(!), our dog's stress is far more straightforward: he loves you and he doesn't want to be apart from you.

In short our holiday times can be very stressful for our dogs, so there are a few things to think about before you dust off your passport, unravel your bikini or dig out your trunks and slather on your factor 25.

Kennels

The majority of pet dogs live in our homes and the change from home to a stay in a kennel can be extreme for some dogs, and very hard to cope with.   If we were taken from our homes and put into a cage with different toileting facilities to those that we're used to, and faced a change of routine, different bed, different rules, and strange noises etc we would understandably find it a little hard. Given some preparation and perhaps the odd practice night away, you can change the experience for the dog. To this end it's important to source the appropriate type of kennel environment for your particular dog. Perhaps see if the kennel can keep the dog to its normal routine as far as possible, perhaps pack some familiar things from home like bedding, toys, chews etc to help them to settle in. It will also make a huge difference if you let the kennel staff know what your dog likes and dislikes, and when it's normally fed and walked etc.

The most important thing is to find holiday care for your dog that is appropriate for its age, state of health, activity levels and individual needs. Try to choose a kennel that isn't too noisy; constant barking and howling may be disturbing for some dogs and the long term downside of this is that your dog may learn to bark and howl from the others. To find a good kennel it can be useful to pick the brains of other dog owners, vets or trainers. Personal recommendation is often a great way to find good places.

If your dog behaves differently on its return home don't worry, changes in behaviour after a period away are usually short-term. Just keep things calm and give them time. Remember the signs of stress and think of how you can make things easier for the dog until it settles down.

Pet Sitters

There are many companies which offer pet-sitting services, this is where someone lives in your home and cares individually for your dog and any other pets. There are many benefits to this including increased security for your home. With a pet sitter your dog never has to leave its home, the dog's routine will remain very similar and it's possibly the least stressful alternative although it may be slightly stressful for the dog to have a stranger living in their home especially the first time. Bear in mind that the dog's response to commands may be different with someone else and ensure that you do a full handover and go on at least one walk with the pet sitter so that they can see how things are normally done.   Always leave the pet sitter a list with emergency contact numbers for your vet, you and perhaps a family member or friend nearby just in case.

Pet Boarding

A home from home for your dog. A professional pet minder will love and care for your dog in their own home giving them the 1:1 attention that they are used to. It would be a good idea before a holiday to go and see the home where the dog will be boarded and go for a walk and discuss your dog's individual requirements, and likes and dislikes etc. Again their own bedding and food will help them to settle in and minimize any tummy upsets. Any sudden change of diet can cause digestive upsets so always ensure that your dog has its own food when away from home; nutritional consistency is important for good health.

NARP (National Association of Registered Pet Sitters) (www.dogsit.com) is a professional organisation that have a register of pet sitters and boarders. There may be others but this is the only one I've found that's national.

Whatever dog care you choose for your particular dog don't leave it to the last minute. Check for appropriate experience, qualifications, memberships, insurances and ideally references. Take the time to make sure your dog has as happy an experience as possible while you are away.

Stress is a vast topic, and the parameters of a book such as this dictate that I can only scratch the surface. But I do highly recommend learning more about stress in both humans and animals. Personally speaking it's truly changed my life and made me happier and healthier, and has done the same for my dogs; so all our lives are even better!

Chapter Six

MENTAL STIMULATION & GAMES TO PLAY

"If you think dogs can't count, try putting three dog biscuits in your pocket and then giving Fido only two of them."

~Phil Pastoret

🐾 Exercising the little grey cells...

Dogs have extremely good brains and are naturally inquisitive, and are interested in life and all that goes with it. So I find it fun and stimulating, for me and for them, to encourage them to learn new things, explore new places and 'exercise the little grey cells' to steal a line from Poirot! When doing any new activities with your dog make it easy for them to understand and give them time to work it out for themselves. If I'm concentrating on something, working or playing a game and someone constantly interrupts me by either trying to make me excited or telling me what to do I would find it irritating and distracting. So remember to be patient and respectful with your dog; try not to speak or direct too much. It's easy to interfere too much and join in verbally or physically with whatever our dogs are doing and sometimes it can be good for them (and us!) if we just stand back and observe quietly.

Set out below are some examples of activities that you can do with your dog that you may not already have thought of but always take into account what your individual dog actually likes to do and bear in mind their state of health, breed, ability and age when considering whether something is, or is not, suitable for your dog.

When doing anything new, and anything with food it's important that you watch your dog to ensure that there is no danger from other dogs or from the materials you are using. I know some owners are concerned about their dogs 'finding food' as an organised game or challenge, as they think it will lead to them scavenging, begging or stealing but that's not my experience. When I set up a game my dogs and client dogs happily go off and find the food but it doesn't seem to lead to scavenging as food that you have placed is OK for them to find and I also teach dogs to leave things that aren't given or placed by me. Dogs with their very good brains can understand the difference between things that are given to them and things that are not.

Play safe and don't forget to use your common sense !

Safety and common sense are important when considering playing, or playing any of the following games. Keep your eyes peeled for clues on your dogs body language and other communication signals; this way you can make sure that your dog doesn't get frustrated, over stimulated or stressed

by the activity. (Note: there are some great books packed with nothing but games for your dog, see recommended reading on pages 104 & 105.) The following ideas are suitable for most dogs of all ages and can be particularly useful for puppies and adolescents. You'll see that 'games' doesn't have to mean just the obvious.

🐾 Scatter Feeding

This is an easy thing to do especially if your dog is on a dry food diet. Food in the bowl can be a bit dull day after day so this livens things up, and injects a little variety into meal times. By scattering your dog's food around the kitchen, garden or on a clean area out on a walk you can find it slows down a dog who usually wolfs his food. So not only will the dog eat more slowly but also the food will last a lot longer. Scattering food has the added advantage of providing stimulation and enables the dog to use it's excellent nose to find it.

However, if you have several dogs be careful that you don't create friction or food guarding by doing this. If you decide to take part of their daily allowance of food out on a walk to scatter somewhere clean do make sure that no other dogs are around. It's often best and safest to do this with dogs individually. In the beginning you won't do this with all of their food, it's something to use occasionally and see if your dog enjoys it. Try not to follow them around pointing out food that they've missed or hurrying them up - sit back and watch quietly. When I scatter food for my dogs I let them know that it's ok to go and get it with a verbal or hand signal.

☸ Hidden Treasure Boxes

Hiding food in throw away items is a great opportunity to put to good use quite a lot of your rubbish (before you throw it away!) for the entertainment of your dog. Plastic bottles such as those that have had milk, water, shampoo or washing up liquid in can be cleaned, rinsed and dried and have treats or dry food put in them. The dog can then work out how to tip them up to get the food out. Make sure that the plastic you use is not the splintering type and that the dog can't come to any harm. Once they've got the food out they quite like to just chew on the plastic, remember dogs love to chew. When doing this sort of activity for the first time watch to make sure that the dog can cope.

Cardboard boxes from light bulbs, cereals, eggs, toiletries etc can all be used, I put either bits of their daily allowance of food in the box or a treat, and then give it to them and they have to either work out how to open the box to get the food out or they have fun ripping open the box. The inner cardboard from kitchen roll or loo roll can also be used all you need to do is push the ends in. Old newspapers can be useful to make a parcel, use your imagination and I'm sure you will come up with some new ideas. Children are often great at thinking up new things to do with rubbish and it can be useful to give dogs something to do if they are bored or you are busy doing something else or going out. Just make sure that you don't make things too difficult for your dog and always consider safety.

☸ Hiding Food (Advanced Scatter Feeding !)

Hiding food is an advance on scatter feeding. It's important that your dog feels confident using his nose to search otherwise he may become confused. When I first taught this to one of my own dogs, I just got him to sit and stay whilst I hid a few bits of food in obvious places only a few feet from him while he was watching then I returned to my dog, rewarded him for the stay, released him and said "*Go find*". Even though he had watched where he put the food he put his nose down and proceeded to find it by scent rather than visually. This is common, dogs tend to prefer to use their sense of smell to locate things. Once your dog understands what "*Go find*" means, you can increase the challenge and hide things in different places and with many variations. When I hide things around the garden these days I hide them up high, underneath pots and in as many creative places as I can think of. My dogs love it, but they're used to it! In the beginning you need to keep it easy. If I've hidden well my dogs will spend ages making sure that they haven't missed any food; going back and re-checking and it may keep them occupied happily for up to half an hour. When the

weather is bad I will utilise different rooms in my home including the cellar and sitting room etc. This may also be done on a walk; when my dogs are finding things they are happily engaged using many of their natural instincts and drives. Again with any new activity don't overdo it, keep it fresh and exciting (but not too exciting!) and observe your dog to make sure that it's happy and coping.

🐾 Finding Items

Instead of throwing a ball or toy for your dog to go and fetch you could hide the item in the bushes and get your dog to go and find it. Again make it easy in the beginning but this is a much better form of exercise for them as they are not rushing madly about. It doesn't put so much strain on them physically and dogs of all ages can do this. Select something that your dog likes and either have someone to hold them while you hide it or get them to sit and stay, remember to always reward the stay before you release them to find the item and keep it calm. Once the dog is confident with this you can vary where you hide the items taking into account what your breed of dog likes to do and is physically capable of. Perhaps up a tree for those dogs that are able to stand on their back legs, for the breeds that like to dig you could bury the item (not too deep) in leaves, loose soil or sand. Try not to verbally encourage them too much or give directions – let them get on with it. Sometimes on a walk I will drop my treat bag and walk on then ask my dogs to find it; they seem to enjoy this occasionally and will rush back and find it for me and then either bring it to me or wait for me to go and pick it up and reward them for their cleverness. There are some great books on nosework and tracking if you want to learn more and you can teach your dog to find anything, people, other dogs, toys, named items etc.

🐾 Treat Tree

This is a lovely way to focus a dog's attention and one of the many activities I learned on summer camps and courses with Sheila Harper and Turid Rugaas. This activity helps slow down an excitable dog and needs to be set up and done without other dogs around. Find a nice tree with low branches and ridged bark and push bits of cheese, pate, dog food or whatever is suitable for your dog into the bark in different places, on the trunk and branches. As your dog gets more experienced with this you can increase the level of difficulty and get the dog to find the tree from a distance away. But in the beginning take your dog to the tree and make it easy for them. If you are having a picnic or a relaxed sit in the park this can provide a happy activity for your dog and whilst they are doing this they tend not to be harassing the local wildlife, wanting to share your picnic or engaging in any other activity that's undesirable.

🐾 Laying a Trail

This is simple and fun. Tie a piece of meat (mine like cooked sausage) or whatever is suitable for your dog onto a piece of string and drag a trail over a clean area away from other dogs. I tend to walk in a large circle and at one point I will stop, break off a piece of the sausage and leave it on the ground then pick up the dragged sausage and put it in a bag in my pocket and then walk back avoiding crossing the trail that I've just made. I will then get my dog and let them follow the trail, they may not follow exactly where you walked as the wind may have carried the scent away from your path but the dog will find its way, keep quiet, keep a loose lead and let them get on with it. This exercise can be done on or off lead, I quite like to do it on lead so that my dog and I are enjoying the activity together, and it ensures they are not distracted by anything else. Ideally use a harness and long lead when following trails for the safety and comfort of your dog.

🐾 Paddling Pools

An ideal and fun way to introduce a dog to water safely. I bought a cheap plastic storage box that's suitable for storing things under the bed so it's shallow for easy access, big enough for the dog to get in and has wheels so that I can move it easily. You only need about four or five inches of water and can make it more fun by throwing treats in for the dog to find. I use things that don't dissolve in the water like cubes of cheese, ham or other meat which sink to the bottom and other treats like puffed jerky that

float. You can also use toys in the water, whatever is suitable for your dog. Whatever you do never force a dog to paddle or swim, give them time to sniff and explore on their own and then they will learn to be confident around water and not suspicious of you. Too many times I've seen people push dogs into ponds or pull them in by their leads and I don't think this is kind or fair.

When out on walks you can play this game in shallow clean areas of water, just take sensible precautions.

W A R N I N G
Toys and Games to Think Twice About

There are some toys and games that you may want to consider with caution. Just as knife juggling is not something you'd encourage in a kindergartener, there are some (less obvious) games for your dog that you need to think twice about. I am unashamedly the fun police when it comes to games that I don't consider to be in a dog's best interests. Many owners who've come to me for training and advice have looked truly horrified when I've suggested they stop playing ball or another favourite game with their dogs. But I'm not being a party pooper, or a spoil sport and nor need you be; where an activity is having a detrimental effect on the behaviour or health of our dogs we owe it to them to do something about it. When I'm working with owners, we explore ideas for a suitable alternative activity to enjoy instead; everyone is happy, including the dogs. You'll find it's surprisingly easy to find better alternatives to the more questionable games.

SQUEEEEEEEEEEEEEEEEEEEEEEAK

Squeaky toys: now obviously I don't know about you but the noise of some of these toys can drive me mad. Remember that our dogs have an excellent and acute sense of hearing; do you think they all enjoy these noises? In actuality squeaky toys can often make dogs quickly over-excited, sometimes destructive and can even cause distress to some (especially some puppies). Any toy that inspires a huge amount of excitement may lead to inappropriate behaviour and an increased likelihood of nipping and jumping up particularly in young or adolescent dogs.

Of course some dogs may be fine and enjoy a squeaky toy or two in a functional way, but consider carefully and watch their reaction and remove the toy if you have any doubts. Many terriers and hunting breeds will find the squeak over-stimulating and tear the toy to bits in a very short space of time! I know of owners who find their dog's (initially much loved) new toy being destroyed within minutes when (for

want of a better example) the squeaky rubber chicken's head has been torn clean off within the first 10 minutes of play. Personally I often to go to charity shops to buy soft toys for my dogs as they don't squeak and ones made for children tend to be safe for dogs as well. But this is not a golden rule; they may not always be safe so you should always check what they are stuffed with and make sure that any bits that could be dangerous are removed.

 TOO MUCH TUG?

Tug games between human and dog are not in my view a great way to interact. If a dog learns to associate someone holding onto an item or picking up an item, with a resulting game of tug they may learn to rush and grab at items picked up by us and others. When they are excited and rushing they may end up inadvertently nipping and grabbing bits of flesh which is definitely not good. Dogs occasionally play tug with each other but generally they stop before it becomes too much. It's worth thinking of

the end result of such games and the level of excitement they cause. Tug games also get the jaws stronger; it's worth bearing in mind that this means that if a dog does bite or nip there is more strength in the muscles. In such cases there is the potential for a dog to literally not have any appreciation of its own strength and really hurt another dog or person.

As you may be aware there is sadly an increase in the use of dogs for fighting. But did you know that one of the ways that they get the dogs' jaws stronger (to enable them to inflict more damage) is to play tug games? They also get the dogs to attack trees and rip off the bark. Another method is to pull down branches for the dogs to get hold of, then the idiot holding the branch lets go; catapaulting the dog into the air. The aim of this cruel, stupid and unkind practice is to get the dogs to bite and not let go. It should go without saying that you should NEVER do this with your dog. Should you have the misfortune to come across anyone doing this type of thing just move away quickly (as you will only endanger yourself and your dog) and phone the local dog warden or RSPCA and report it.

ANYONE FOR TENNIS?

The tennis ball launchers on the market can be great for some dogs if used sensibly. (You know the ones: theres a tennis ball grasped in a long handled scoop which helps owners to launch tennis balls far greater distances than they could with a simple throw.) In this context I use the term 'sensibly' to mean 'very occasionally'; once a week maximum... if you really have to! The problem is that these launchers can be a lazy option for owners, and be options that actually provide inappropriate exercise for certain dogs. Recently I saw an extremely lame dog walk onto my local common, he was taken off lead and he started sniffing around slowly and ambling about. Then his owner got out the tennis ball and its launcher and this stiff and lame dog suddenly got a crazed look in his eye and started jumping and running like a much younger and fitter dog. I was leaving the park but waited and observed the game go on for over 10 minutes; the dog was unquestionably over-stimulated. Now I know I'm not a vet but I am also confident that this exercise was not in the dog's best interests either physically or mentally. Once adrenaline kicks in, pain is not felt so much, but the underlying problem hasn't changed and may become worse. Thus a dog who goes from gently walking to full-on running and jumping with little or no warm up can suffer serious ill effects. The next day (when the adrenaline has worn off and the muscles are recovering) the dog will feel a great deal more pain and discomfort than before they went out for their 'fun game'. In some cases whilst they are running about madly they may be causing themselves harm and they certainly aren't socialising, sniffing or attending to proper dog stuff.

Once in a while for short periods of time if the dog is in a fit physical state this type of exercise can be OK, but consider what you want to achieve through this type of game. It's not uncommon for dogs that 'love to play ball' in park to pull on lead all the way to the park or bark and whine in the car on the way to the park. I sometimes liken the use of this sort of exercise to me going to park suddenly running around like a maniac until I'm really sweating and exhausted then going home to lie in bed for the rest of the day!! Not sure I'd feel great without a warm up, cool down or if it went on day after day.

 FETCH

In many ways this discussion is an extension of the previous tennis ball one. Though to be clear I am not against fetch per se. All I will say is this: if you do want to play fetch games with your dog keep the sessions short and don't throw the ball when other dogs are about as this can result in competition and perhaps conflict. It's not uncommon for a dog that is chasing a ball to fail to notice another dog coming up behind them. I've witnessed dogs run up and nip or bite a dog chasing a ball. There are plenty of

possible of explanations for this: it could be that the dog thinks that the ball chaser is behaving in rude way in dog terms, or it could have triggered a prey/chase response in the chasing dog. Whatever the cause a game that risks your dog being nipped or bitten by another dog is not a good thing! When a dog has had an exciting play session it will be in a heightened state emotionally and more prone to over-react. I've had various clients over the years who have commented that their dog becomes grumpy with other dogs after playing ball, but there's an easy solution, don't play ball

and if you do don't do it too often and avoid other dogs afterwards. Alternatively play occasionally (once a week or less) for a short while. Make this just one chunk of a playtime session with your dog; play other games, enjoy quality time together and don't just rely on a single game to stimulate your dog physically or mentally.

 STICKS

Now brace yourselves, because after my harsh words about the 'classic' dog games of tug and fetch, we're coming to sticks! Of course dogs choose to chew sticks sometimes and I'm not saying you have to stop them, it's fine to just let them get on with it on their own, but equally if you don't want them to stick munch, and if you're not happy you should distract them away. Throwing sticks or playing tug with sticks *can* genuinely be dangerous for dogs. It's very easy for splinters of wood to get into their gums and cause infections, abscesses and damage teeth. Even worse: the stick (or splinters from it) can get stuck in the gullet or pierce the inside of the mouth.

FRISBEES

Sorry to be a Fun Policeman again but many of the hard plastic Frisbees can damage the dog's teeth and gums. On the more positive side though if you look out for the soft ones, these are much safer and far less likely to harm your dog when he catches it. So you'll be able to frisbee away together happily! (Again bearing in mind all the usual precautions about your dog's state of health etc, and of course only playing from time to time.)

🐾 PLAYTIME TIPS

🐾 With all the above games remember: one dog, one task.

🐾 Plan what you're going to do and how you're going to do it.

🐾 Don't repeat the same game over and over and over and over, again and again and again and again. (Repetition gets monotonous doesn't it...?!) If we overdo any game the dog will stop enjoying it and become over-tired, bored or stressed.

🐾 Space out activities sensibly so you're neither doing something completely different, nor something exactly the same every single day and have rest days between different activities.

🐾 Attempting too many tasks can be over stimulating, confusing and tiring for you and your dog.

🐾 If you do any activity as a family plan together and remember to be consistent with any verbal cues. Have only one person working with or directing the dog at a time. And try not to get *yourselves* over-excited or stressed!

🐾 Think about how much you speak to the dog when doing any game, or even when out walking generally or at home. Constant chatter can sometimes be distracting and stressful, and you can even find your dog tunes out and ends up ignoring you.

🐾 Because weather is so unpredictable you can't usually *plan* to play in the snow or splash about in puddles, but you can make the most of these things when they happen. Most dogs love a good wallow in some mud or bouncing through the snow, but remember not to force them and to introduce them to new sensations gently, with thought and care.

With care and planning you can set yourself and your dog up for fun and success with all your endeavours.

We can affect the outcome of games, training and our relationship with our dogs by the way we speak to them, the way we touch them and the exercise we give them.

Enjoy your life with your dog and try to keep a sensible balance: have a lovely long walk in the woods, do some tracking and games on the weekend but then have a quiet few days afterwards. Go to the dog show or training class but remember to keep it calm for the following several days or longer depending on the dog.

Think about how much training you do and ask yourself: is it perhaps too much sometimes? Personally I find that a training class every 2 weeks is enough for my dogs and me, as we tend to enjoy to do many other things and I'm conscious of not doing too much. Experiment with different activities with your dog where appropriate, and make sure the dog has time to recover emotionally and physically from each event.

Remember, fun and games should be fun! Just make sure you think about what you're doing, and think about the who, what, when, wheres and hows, and most of all make sure you and your dog enjoy yourselves!

Chapter Seven

EXERCISE

"If your dog is fat, you're not getting enough exercise."

~ Anon

Exercise of dogs is important but it should be appropriate exercise dependent on breed, age and state of health.

Woof Woof
Ruff
(Dog Exercise
Area)

New Zealanders like to think they can speak dog

🐾 **3 month old puppy?** A generally accepted rule of thumb is to walk a puppy of 3 months for 15 minutes at a time, once a day in the beginning, going slowly and allowing them to explore and sniff.

🐾 **For each month beyond 3 months?** For each month add another 5 minutes to the walk so at 4 months you will be out for approximately 20 minutes at a time and so by 5 months you'll be out for 25 minutes. Keep adding 5 minutes per month until you are walking for the amount of time that suits you *and* the dog.

🐾 **Sitting down? Getting over excited?** If you notice your puppy sitting down a lot or getting over excited it could be that you need to reduce the length and regularity of the walks.

🐾 **Up to 3 times a day?** How many times a day you walk your dog is really down to you and your dog. However there isn't really any need to walk dogs more than 3 times a day. I generally walk mine twice a day, except on tired days when they need to rest and it might be just one short slow walk.

🐾 **Weekend expeditions... complemented by short and sweet weekdays:** Quite often my dogs have the choice of where we go and for how long, they're pretty sensible and enjoy the choice sometimes. Obviously we all do longer walks sometimes especially at weekends and when the weather is lovely, but after a longer more stimulating and tiring walk it's a good idea to keep the walks shorter and calmer for the following few days.

🐾 **Take care not to overdo it:** With all dogs (but particularly bigger breeds) you need to take care not to over-exercise when they are young as you could be affecting their growth and development and potentially be setting them up for problems when they are older. Jumping and prolonged running is definitely not suitable for young dogs and puppies, or for many of the bigger breeds.

🐾 **Know your stuff**: Research your breed and if in doubt speak to your vet, trainer or breeder about what's suitable and safe in terms of exercise.

🐾 **Variety is the spice of life**: Varying your walks occasionally in terms of length, area and time of day will keep things more interesting for you and your dog.

🐾 **On Lead?** I like to let my dogs off lead but they certainly don't get to run off lead on every walk. Walking nicely on lead takes practice and patience so if you always have your dog off lead in the park it will never learn to walk well on the lead. I don't insist on my dogs walking to heel but I like them to walk on a loose lead near to me, and I will intersperse lead walking and off lead walking in the park so that their expectation isn't always to be free in the park.

If the only time you use the lead is to go to the park and then (when the time is up), you catch your dog and put the lead on and go home... well, then, the dog may learn to see the lead as a negative and start to not come back to you. This has happened in many cases that I've seen. Another problem that can arise is when the owner gets the dog to the park, then lets the dog off lead and the dog whizzes off running around playing with other dogs. These dogs can actually sometimes feel ignored by their owners, and they in turn begin to ignore their owners, and before you know it these dogs don't want to leave the park. But if you think about it, if you went for a walk with a friend and they spent all of their time on the far side of the park not interacting with you, and just ignoring you, you'd be a little upset. When I walk with my dogs I prefer them to be with me or to check in regularly. Obviously I want them to have a good time and to meet other dogs but for reasons of safety I like them to be nearby and in sight for the majority of the time.

🐾 **How and where to go?** What's acceptable to you and how and where you walk your dog will depend on the area in which you live. I love where I live in central London, as I have several lovely parks within easy walking distance which are all different in style, plus pretty river paths along by the Thames only a 10 minute walk away. There are a number of local pubs, bars and cafes

Morning coffee

that welcome dogs, provide water (and even treats in some cases) so a walk can in fact include having coffee, lunch, drinks or dinner which adds to the fun and variety. I can choose to walk in busy areas but also know where to go where I won't actually see anyone else or any other dogs. This can be a real advantage; as some days we all need quiet time.

Dogs don't always need to be on grass, or in a park to have a good time, mine actually like to walk past the local waste and

Exploring together by the Thames

recycling depot extremely slowly with their noses exploring all the smells in the air and on the ground. They can have a fabulously interesting time on lead walking through this small industrial area. Use your imagination and try to think about what your dog might like in the way of a different walk.

Social walks

Social walks are a great way for you and your dogs to exercise, socialise and have a lovely learning experience together. When I organise a social walk with clients or friends I think about the needs of the different dogs in the group based on their breed and age, and how comfortable they are with other dogs, plus I consider their energy levels and experience.

The general aim of the social walks that I organise is for less confident or inexperienced dogs and owners, to gain good experience of being with others in a calm and enjoyable way. And also to improve their social skills, coping ability and learn good things from each other.

To start with, and certainly for the first few walks, all dogs are on lead and owners must have some knowledge of calming signals. Thus they recognise when it's necessary to increase distance from another dog, turn away when appropriate and they recognise when their dog has had enough and take them home.

🐾 **Group size**: How large or small the group should be depends very much on how each dog in the group can cope, as we want to ensure that it's an enjoyable and functional experience.

🐾 **Puppy or dog's first social walk: who to invite?** The first social walk that a puppy or dog goes on will be with only one, or perhaps two other dogs, who are ideally experienced at walking with others. We need to set the dogs and owners up for success and choose an area where there is plenty of space and without too many other people around. Plan and choose times and places that will provide the most ideal situation. Make sure that you have dogs in the group who are capable of getting along and owners who are confident and able in their handling skills.

🐾 **Length**: The first walk should not be too long so if there is a 4 month old puppy in the group the walk should be no longer than about 20 minutes or so. In fact even with adult dogs in the beginning I would keep the walks to a maximum of about 40 minutes in length.

I always love to see dogs interacting with each other and I constantly learn more about them by observing them in groups. Good social experiences where dogs learn to cope with a variety of situations and practice their communication in a relaxed way enables your dog to better deal with some of the not so good experiences that inevitably happen from time to time. If most of their experiences are good ones they will be able to recover from the odd negative one quickly and will in fact have the skills to be able defuse potentially difficult encounters.

Social walk with friends

Bear in mind that many dogs that I see as clients with behavioural problems have either too much or the wrong type of exercise so it's important to get it right for your individual dog and for you.

SUPER BASIC TRAINING

This book isn't about training as such but I'm including some basic training techniques and thoughts that you might find helpful.

🐾 **Recall** is, I think, one of the most important things we teach our dogs. If your dog doesn't come back to you when called, then whether it can sit, lie down or jump through hoops is fairly irrelevant. A fast and happy recall provides an opportunity for your dog to run free and I prefer mine to run towards me rather than away from me!

There are various ways to teach a good recall and I tend to start by teaching them on lead so that the opportunity for them to get it wrong or misunderstand is limited. As I'm walking along with the dog on a long loose lead I call their name to get their attention and start to walk backwards saying "Come, come" in a friendly and encouraging way. The fact that you're moving slowly away from them will make you attractive to come towards. As soon as they get to me I reward them. I use good quality treats that the dog finds motivating for the recall. It's important to reward immediately and don't ask them to sit or do anything else or you end up rewarding the sit and not the recall. Keep it simple and easy for them.

It's useful to practice the recall in the house and garden and in many different situations using the same method (not necessarily on lead in the house and garden unless you need to):

🐾 First call their name then "Come, come" or whatever word or phrase you choose to use.

🐾 Move away from the dog as it approaches to make yourself more appealing and exciting to come towards. (You can crouch down or turn sideways on as well which makes also you more appealing to come towards; remember canine communication and make yourself an attractive and happy owner to come back to.)

🐾 In the early stages practice with as few distractions as possible. Set your dog up for success, make it fun and don't overdo the practice.

With time and practice you can establish a great recall but bear in mind that when your dog is interacting with another dog they may not come back immediately; they'll need to finish their social encounter first, before returning to you otherwise they risk seeming rude and offending the other dog. If we were in a conversation with another person and we suddenly just turned and walked away mid sentence when someone called us it wouldn't be very polite. Dogs prefer to communicate their peaceful intentions and avoid conflict, so give them a chance to act on your request and finish what they're doing first. The recall will be unsuccessful if your dog is over-excited or deeply engrossed in something else. I sometimes run away from my dogs or hide from them to make coming back to me more exciting.

This is only a basic approach to recall but there are many books out there on training if you want to go into it in more detail (see pages 104 & 105).

🐾 Walking nicely on lead

As I've mentioned above I don't really want my dogs to walk to heel and am happy for them to walk in a relaxed way beside, ahead or behind me; whatever suits them. Personally I also prefer my dogs to wear a well fitting flat harness and use a longer than normal lead.

🐾 To set yourself up for a relaxed walk prepare for the walk and leave the house in a calm and gentle way, if the dog starts to get excited just stop what you're doing and wait for them to calm down. They need to learn that the only way to get out of the door is slowly and calmly.

🐾 Once out on the street I praise and talk to my dogs when they are walking close to me and stop and stand still when they pull ahead, when I stop they tend to look back at me and come back towards me and then I move again.

🐾 Note: There are a great many ways to teach walking on a loose lead and different methods work with different dogs but jerking your dog around isn't a kind or effective way to do it. There are many training aids and devices on the market to help you if your dog pulls but really the only way to get a dog that walks nicely on lead is to practice. There is no better way to improve (at anything) than practice.

Healthy + well balanced = receptive to learning: A dog that is healthy and well balanced emotionally and physically will be easier to teach, and such dogs are less likely to pull.

Pulling? Puppies pull and jerk about on the lead in the beginning as everything is so new and exciting, it's like trying to take a small child into a big toy store and expect them to walk slowly, listen to you and be calm! Give them time to explore, and be patient but persistent.

Adolescents of all species can be difficult: Adolescents can be challenging and pull on lead and generally have good days and bad days training wise. To be honest it is best to try to ignore some adolescent behaviour and trust that with a calm and consistent approach they will grow out of it. The good thing about adolesence in dogs is that it's over in a relatively short period of time. When I felt frustrated with my own young dog I just looked at some of the teenagers on the street and in the shopping malls and realised that actually she wasn't that bad!

Extra excited? It's normal for dogs to be more excited some days and to be more stimulated in new areas, I liken it to trying to get one of my fashionable shopaholic friends to walk slowly, listen to me and be calm when their favourite shop has a huge sale on: not a hope!

Have realistic expectations: Don't expect too much from your dog; we all make mistakes and can get distracted, and we all have good and bad days, so it's only fair that we accept that our dogs do too.

Remember that there are many, many different ways to train a dog and it's about finding the method that suits you and your dog, I'm uncomfortable when people say 'you must' when it comes to types of training. Clicker training has its place but it's not for everyone, classes are useful for some but its individual and there are many dogs that struggle to cope with the noise and close proximity of other dogs in a confined space. I've observed classes where once in the hall the dog behaves in an exemplary and obedient manner, but out on the street they pull on lead and have inter-dog problems. I wonder if class is the right place for that particular type of dog to learn essential skills.

Take time to stop and enjoy the peace when walking

Training is a massive subject and it's not really necessary to train your dog to do everything on command, I prefer to teach my dogs to cope with a variety of different situations and to be equipped to be able to make good decisions themselves so that I don't have to tell them what to do. Over the years a great many rigid rules have been taught to owners when it comes to dogs and the implication is that if you don't follow them you will have problems, I don't believe this is so. I prefer my dogs to walk through doorways ahead of me so that I can see them safely through, I feed them at times that suit them and me and I don't think that they think less of me if I don't bother to make a point of eating something before I feed them. They choose where they sleep in my home, there are beds in every room and they can suit themselves but that's what suits me, what suits you in terms of training and living with your dog is up to you.

Boundaries and rules are useful; if you had a relationship with a partner and they didn't mind what you did at all... not ever... you may well feel that they actually didn't care. So in all relationships, including those with our dogs, sensible boundaries and a consistent approach are fairly essential. But as with all rules breaking or relaxing them now and again is OK in *some* circumstances. You don't need to enforce them rigidly all the time.

In essence if your dog is healthy, relaxed and balanced and is capable of making it's own good decisions sometimes, then you will have a very happy time and you'll have got your 'training' right.

Chapter Eight

HEALTH & NUTRITION

🐾 **Good health**: there are a great many factors that create a state of good health and we've already talked about several of them. Nutrition is a factor in health and can also be a factor in many problem behaviours. I'm not a canine nutritionist but I do have a huge interest and good working knowledge of human nutritional therapy and have attended several courses and read many books on canine nutrition.

There are a few common sense things to bear in mind; nutrition can be a highly emotional subject with a lot of bold statements such as *'this is the only way to feed your dog'* and *'you must...'*. With any of these types of statement I want to know where the facts come from and what current, unbiased and professional scientific work backs up the claims. Every dog is an individual and their nutritional requirements will change throughout their lives depending on their age, health, exercise levels, breed and gender. Different breeds may do better on some particular types of diet than others but it's important that your dog's diet is suitable for its individual requirement at each stage of its life and provides appropriate and complete nutrition.

🐾 **Good quality nutrition**: the ideal is a good quality nutritionally complete diet that suits you and your dog in terms of price, convenience and palatability. If the dog doesn't like it it's possibly not the right diet. If in doubt speak to your vet, there is generally someone in the practice who has an interest and knowledge of nutrition and they can advise you. Alternatively you can find a qualified canine nutritionist who can give you impartial advice and guidance. We know that it's not healthy for our dogs to be overweight and it's also not healthy for them to be too thin either. As in the human world of food there is good healthy food and the canine version of junk food. A bit of junk food isn't the end of the world occasionally although some dogs might be sensitive to any dietary changes or treats so it's worth basing what you feed on the individual dog. I eat a healthy balanced diet that suits me but what suits me may not suit you, and what suits my dogs may not suit your dogs so it really is worth making sure that you find the right diet for your dog and one that it enjoys.

What to look for: when it comes to quality I read ingredients on the packs and personally I prefer not to feed foods that include derivatives whether animal, vegetable or fish in origin. If you want to know what these 'derivatives' are it's very easy with a very quick search to find information on the internet. Having done so then you can make an informed decision as to whether or not you want to pay money for them as an ingredient. Remember that price isn't the key indicator of quality, though it is fair to say that some of the high quality foods are more expensive. Personally I do choose to pay a slightly higher price for a good quality food with good quality ingredients as I feel that in the long term it makes sense and will help to give my dogs good long term health. (And if one was being financially driven it's worth remembering that a healthy dog is far less likely to have horrid health horrors that lead to vast vet's bills.)

Colourings: some dog foods contain food colourings, and on the basis that research has shown that dogs don't take colour into account when they eat, I personally see no benefit to colouring dog food. There are many scientific reports linking the consumption of artificial colourings to behavioural problems in children, and using common sense that must surely have implications for us and our dogs consuming such colourings.

There is much anecdotal evidence from trainers and dog owners to suggest that certain foods with additives and colourings have caused their dogs to become hyperactive or aggressive (amongst other problems). When these same dogs switched to additive and colourant free foods the dogs changed completely, and the problems disappeared. Don't be fooled by the fact that your dog may love the additive filled foods; look at their whole behaviour. Afterall many children love chewy sweets, chocolate bars and cola, but once you've experienced a group of five year olds bouncing off the walls in a hyper and emotionally charged sugar rush you'd think twice before allowing them unlimited access to those 'treats' again wouldn't you? Personally I know I've experienced short term detrimental changes in my health and general comfort as a result of eating artificially coloured food items: I definitely didn't enjoy the experience!

Thus in my opinion I don't think it's advisable to give your dogs food containing artificial colourings. I have yet to identify a nutritional value to colouring dog food or a good reason for them to be used in the manufacture of dog food or treats (other for them to look more appealing to the human eye when we're making our buying decision).

🐾 **Sugar**: sugar is not ideal in a dog's diet. If they are unlucky enough to need dental work it requires a general anaesthetic which is not without risk. Sugar has no nutritional value for dogs and seems only to potentially have a detrimental and long term effect on teeth and health. There is much written about how bad sugar is for dogs (let alone people) and if you want to find out more, again a cursory internet search will provide you with more information that you couldn't possibly hope to read in its entirety! Having boned up on the detrimental effects of sugar (and sorbitol (but that's a whole other can of worms)) you will hopefully be put off ever thinking about giving it to your dog. Make sure you check your food labels as a surprising number of dog foods and treats contain sugar and/or sorbitol.

🐾 **Switching your dog's diet**: it's tricky to know which of the 'good diets' is best for your dog. You can test out different foods and look at your dog's coat, skin, weight and what's going on inside (usually a good clue being what comes out). Dandruff, itchiness, bad odours, hyperactivity and sluggishness (to name just a few problems) can frequently be corrected with a change of diet. Epileptic dogs have even been known to reduce the frequency of their seizures simply by switching to natural and hypoallergenic diets. Do remember that if you have discovered that the food you have been giving your dog isn't up to scratch and you want to switch him to a better quality food, he may well react just the same as a child would if you switched them from regular snacks laden with sugar, salt and flavourings to 'delicious and nutritious' carrot sticks and rice cakes. Don't be alarmed or disheartened if your dog is not keen at first. Introduce changes gradually and persistence will win out; though you may need to test to find the right food for your dog. If in doubt your veterinary surgery will almost certainly be able to offer you great advice.

🐾 **General thoughts and tips on health and nutrition**: there are a great many different ways to feed your dog and many interesting and informative books on the subject so it's worth thinking about how you're going to feed your dog, and be consistent. If you don't know what's in it , then preferably don't give it to your dog. Health is about balance. So have a balanced approach and a balanced diet and you won't go far wrong (and that applies to both you and your dog!)

       ...and whilst we're talking about 'balance'... As a human and canine Bowen therapist I think that it's a wonderful and balancing complementary therapy for both people, dogs and horses. On the next couple of pages there is a little information about it. Complementary therapy is used on animals in conjunction with appropriate veterinary care and is never practised without veterinary referral. There are other complementary therapies which can be very effective for dogs including, homeopathy, flower essences, nutritional therapy and essential oil therapy.

A thought provoking point about animals and complementary therapy is that there is no placebo effect: dogs have no expectation... so either they improve or they don't... it works or doesn't. It would be nigh on impossible to say it's all mind over matter when it comes to animals.

Canine Bowen Technique

🐾 **What is it?** Canine Bowen Technique is a hands-on remedial therapy. It's different to many other complementary therapies as it involves a series of gentle rolling type moves made on different parts of the body. There are rest periods in between moves to allow the body to process the effects of each series of moves. The Bowen moves can promote healing, and help to re-balance and re-align the body. It can offer pain relief for a variety of conditions, increase joint mobility, provide opportunity for relaxation and may help with energy levels. The Bowen Technique is a very effective therapy for people and horses as well as dogs, but it is of course important that you choose a therapist who is specifically qualified for the required field (human, canine or equine) to ensure the best and safest treatment.

🐾 **What types of condition can it help?** Firstly, Canine Bowen Technique treats the whole body not just named conditions or symptoms. It can help to alleviate a wide range of problems including; joint pain and stiffness, breathing difficulties, tension and stress. In addition it can enhance sports performance, aid recovery from surgery and illness, help with muscular strains & sprains, and with auto-immune disorders and can contribute to overall good health which may help to reduce the likelihood of injury or illness in all dogs, and particularly working or competition dogs.

🐾 **How many sessions will the dog need?** This will vary very much on the dog and the overall condition but generally after one or two sessions some change should be observed. It's often a good idea to have maintenance sessions to aid prevention of injury or illness and promote good general health. Most commonly the sessions take place in the dog's own home.

🐾 **Is it safe?** Canine Bowen Technique is very safe as it's so gentle and it's never forced on a dog. Canine Bowen is only ever practised on a dog following veterinary referral and it's important to ensure that your Canine Bowen Technique Therapist is qualified, insured and attends annual CPD (continued professional development) courses to remain up-to-date and effective.

🐾 **What will happen during the session?** Firstly, the Canine Bowen Technique Therapist will take a full history of the dog and observe the dog moving, sitting, standing and lying (where appropriate) and also note any medication that the dog is on and what veterinary advice you have been given. The therapist may want to know about the dog's life, daily routine, diet and exercise to help them to see the whole picture. Once a visual and physical observation has been done the therapist will proceed with the treatment taking care to ensure the dog's comfort at all times. The therapist will assess the dog between the moves and at the end of the session.

🐾 **How do I find a Canine Bowen Technique Therapist?**
Either through the European Guild of Canine Bowen Therapists (www.caninebowentechnique.com) or the Bowen Therapists' European Register (www.bter.org).

There is no doubt that the Canine Bowen Technique is a fabulous and effective therapy for dogs and my respect for dogs deepens every time one allows me to do Bowen on them. Instinctively many dogs know when they've had enough Bowen for one session, they know when they need a break and where they want the moves to be done: very often they control the session in an instinctive and wise way.

Just a Handful of Real Life Canine Bowen Success Stories

Before: 4 yr old cocker spaniel who had very low energy, intermittent lameness in all legs, difficulty walking, climbing stairs and getting up from a sit/down position. Veterinary tests had been inconclusive in diagnosing what was wrong.

After: After one session the dog was able to get up from sit/down position unaided, had more energy and became a young dog again. After a second session the dog appeared to be normal and has continued to lead an active and happy life.

Before: 12 month old lurcher was nervous and exhibited destructive chewing behaviour after being spayed.

After: After one session she was more relaxed and didn't chew anything that wasn't hers. She had a second session and became her normal confident and well adjusted self. She also healed very quickly.

Before: 8 yr old Labrador bruised his back going under a gate on a day out shooting, his back was painful to touch and he appeared stiff and sore when he walked.

After: He had one session and then slept, the next day he walked easily, was sound and didn't mind his back being touched.

...AND FINALLY...

The subject of dogs is immense and leads on to so many other fascinating and related subjects that I have learned to love learning more than ever. I constantly strive to find out more about humans and dogs in terms of behaviour, motivation, communication, health, nutrition, training, mental stimulation, fitness and relationships; in fact generally how to enjoy life more.

Sharing life with my dogs and working with dogs and their owners has been and continues to be hugely rewarding. And a really surprising side effect of learning more about dogs is that I learned more about me. Over the past few years I've been lucky enough to have been able to make some really positive changes in my life and am now happier, more fulfilled and healthier than I've ever been. If anyone had predicted that in my 40s I would become a 'mad old dog woman' I would have laughed but in fact it's the best thing I've ever done. I hope you and your dogs have many happy years eating, drinking, playing, learning, communicating, thinking, resting and basically just living together.

In essence, I hope that in some small way I have helped you learn a little more about the great pleasure (for both you and your dog) that can be be derived from knowing *How to Handle Living With Your Dog*.

Further Information and Recommended Reading

Below are just a few sources of information and books that I've enjoyed. I can highly recommend buying or borrowing some of the books and going on courses to learn more.

🐾 **Sheila Harper** teaches a very comprehensive course: 'International Dog Behaviour & Training School'. She also offers many weekend courses on a large variety of dog related subjects. Check out her website for more information:
www.sheilaharper.co.uk

🐾 **Sally Askew**: Founder of European Guild of Canine Bowen Therapists, Trainer/Behaviourist, Small Animal Nutritionist and Essential Oil Therapist for Dogs. Sally, along with her husband Ron, teaches the Canine Bowen Technique in the UK and abroad. She also conducts courses on Canine Nutrition, Health & Behaviour. For more information go to:
www.caninebowentechnique.com

🐾 **Turid Rugaas** - Turid does a variety of wonderful talks, summer camps and courses in the UK and around the World, it's well worth going to see her if you get the chance. Two of Turid's publications I'd recommend particularly are listed below under 'Great Dog Books'.
www.turid-rugaas.no/UKFront.htm
(This is the UK homepage rather than the Norwegian one!)

Great Dog Books

🐾 **Canine Nutrition**
  Lowell Ackerman

🐾 **Minding Animals**
  Marc Bekoff

🐾 **Give Your Dog a Bone**
  Ian Billinghurst

🐾 **Bones Would Rain from the Sky**
  Suzanne Clothier

🐾 **Dogs**
  Raymond and Lorna Coppinger

🐾 **How Dogs Think**
Stanley Coren

🐾 **The Culture Clash**
Jean Donaldson

🐾 **Wild Health**
Cindy Engel

🐾 **Why Does my Dog?**
John Fisher

🐾 **Think Dog**
John Fisher

🐾 **When Pets Come Between Partners**
Joelle Gavrielle-Gold

🐾 **Fun Nosework for Dogs**
Roy Hunter

🐾 **The Other End of the Leash**
Patricia B McConnell

🐾 **Food Pets Die For**
Ann N Martin

🐾 **Dominance Theory - Fact or Fiction**
James O'Heare

🐾 **Lads Before the Wind**
Karen Pryor

🐾 **On Talking Terms with Dogs: Calming Signals** (book & video)
Turid Rugaas

🐾 **What do I do when my dog pulls?**
Turid Rugaas

🐾 **Why Zebra's Don't Get Ulcers**
Robert Sapowlsky

🐾 **Dogs That Know When Their Owners Are Coming Home**
Rupert Sheldrake

🐾 **Playtime for your Dog**
Christina Sondemann

Useful Links

www.bowentherapists.com
The Bowen Technique European Register to find canine, equine or human Bowen Therapists.

www.sheilaharper.co.uk
For wonderful in depth short courses of 1 to 10 days and longer term accredited professional training, quality equipment; harnesses and leads, toys, treats and an excellent range of books.

www.learningaboutanimals.co.uk
Provides information and promotes interest in the welfare and behaviour of animals by holding various events throughout the year.

www.dog-games.co.uk
For good quality and well fitting harnesses and long leads.

www.fish4dogs.com
Fishy treats for dogs that contain only natural ingredients.

www.apdt.co.uk
Association of Pet Dog Trainers: go to their website to find a dog trainer in your area. All members of the APDT have been assessed according to a strict code of practice and have agreed to abide by kind and fair principles of training. To this end the use of coercive or punitive techniques and equipment are not used.

www.pet-dog-trainers-europe.org
The Pet Dog Trainers of Europe (PDTE) is an international organisation. Full members must meet strict criteria and commit to continuing professional development. The PDTE promotes the best possible practices in training and places great emphasis on the importance of canine communication.

www.kongcompany.com
For guidance on kong toys, size guidance and recipe ideas for kong stuffings. (Note: Kongs are available worldwide from pet stores, and pet sections of stores. You cannot buy direct from the Kong website.)

www.winkiespiers.com
My website providing further information about the treaments I offer, and classes, sessions and talks I am running, and also providing my contact details and other useful links.

Enjoyed Winkie's book?
Why not order more copies for your
friends online! Just go to:

www.shortstackpublishing.com

Other titles in the series:
**How to Handle Your Recruitment
Consultant**

Forthcoming Short Stack Titles
How to Handle Christmas
How to Handle Your Wedding
How to Handle Burns Night
How to Handle Being a Newlywed
How to Handle Rejection
How to Handle TTC
How to Handle a Mid Life Crisis

Printed in the United States
1318LVUK00001B